# ANONYMOUS

## NAMING THE GOD OF ESTHER

### AND

## THE WOMEN WHO PLANT CHURCHES

DORI GORMAN

WITH SARA MCGUE

Cover & interior design by Lena Masek (lenamasek.website).

ISBN-13: 978-1544263908
ISBN-10: 1544263902

# DEDICATED TO MY DAUGHTERS

Charis and Nia, may you never forget that God has an incredible plan for each of your lives. Rather than telling me what it is, Jesus wants to tell you and invite you to join his work in the world. It is my job, in partnership with your amazing dad, to teach you how to hear the Spirit's voice. I pray you listen well as you grow into your names with both grace and purpose.

"Coincidences are God's way
of remaining anonymous."

**DORIS LESSING**
*Nobel Prize-winning author*

# CONTENTS

ANONYMOUS

# MY NAME IS...

My name is Dori. But that's not always the name I wanted. Long before *Finding Nemo* and Ellen Degeneres made my name popular, there were many names I wanted rather than Dori. For some unknown reason I went through a season in 1st grade where I signed all of my papers "Dor." That's right. Just drop the "i" and call me "Dor." I have no earthly idea why I thought this was cool. Thankfully it didn't last long. My brother started calling me "Window" and I realized that having "Dor" as a nickname wouldn't actually make me popular.

After my "Dor" phase I went through a "Jason" period. I have always been a bit of a tomboy. I preferred playing football, climbing trees and picking scabs over wearing dresses, doing my hair and anything associated with the color pink. That's why I dreaded the annual intergenerational tea party hosted by my grandmother every December. The ritual was set: the women of our family would cook all morning, decorate the house and get dressed up—all for the purpose of drinking tea and talking with other dressed-up women. Needless to say, I didn't get it.

Just before the tea started, the women in my family would gather in the living room for a picture. We would then turn and take a picture of the men as well. But their picture was more of a joke. They weren't dressed fancy or anything. No, the men were comfortable in their blue jeans and t-shirts ready to go to the hardware store, the movies, McDonalds or other adventurous 'man' places.

By 3rd grade I decided enough was enough. After my mom finished helping me get dressed and ready, I went to my suitcase and did what any true-blooded tomboy would do. I put on my blue jeans and my t-shirt. I pulled my perfectly fixed up hair into a lop-sided ponytail. And then I hid. Because that's what you do when you're a tomboy at a tea party.

The time finally arrived for the pictures to be taken and I was nowhere to be found. "Dori? Where are you? Dori!" I could hear my name being called throughout the house. That's when I made my move. I walked into the living room, marched up to my mom and boldly proclaimed, "My name is Jason and I'm going with the men." This picture perfectly sums up the look and swagger I was going for with that proclamation.

Of course, after the laughter died down, I was marched back to my suitcase where my dress was waiting for me. This picture shows how I actually looked before the guests arrived and the tea party started. After all, my name was Dori and I was sticking with the women.

So here I am today, many years later. I have learned to like my name and to like being a woman. My name is Dori and I am a church planter. My husband, Rich, and I moved to Chicago in December of 2010 to start a church on the north side of the city in one of the most diverse zip codes in the United States. It has been, and continues to be, the most awe-inspiring, gut-wrenching, grievous, joyous thing we have ever been called by God to do. This book comes out of our experiences together as co-pastors of NewStory Church in Chicago (newstorychicago.com).

Like many churches, every season we encourage our congregation to be a part of a small group. In the winter of 2016 I was given the opportunity to co-lead a women's Small Group on the book of Esther—some of the women who were a part of this group are pictured here. Throughout this small group season I began to notice parallels between the women in our group and the stories of Vashti, Esther, Mordecai, Haman and Ahasuerus. Esther is the only book in the Bible that does not have the name "God" in it. There is no mention of "elohim" or "yayweh" in the entire book. I guess you could say God is anonymous in Esther. But in other ways that isn't true at all. God's handprint is seen throughout the book in countless coincidences and nuances. My life is like that sometimes. God hasn't spoken to me through a burning bush. I haven't touched the scarred hands of Jesus. God seems anonymous. By faith, however, I believe God is real. God is living and active. God is moving and if I raise my sails at the right time, God moves me.

One day I shared these thoughts with a friend and mentor from Stadia. Stadia (stadia.cc) is the church planting organization which helped start NewStory. Specifically, I was talking with Debbie Jones who leads Bloom, a ministry of Stadia that intentionally empowers women to maximize their role in starting churches (stadia.cc/bloom). It was Debbie who first helped me see how the anonymity of God within the stories of Esther connected with the stories of church planting women.

As a female church planter in Chicago I have not felt anonymous. I am incredibly blessed to have Rich as my husband. He sees me as an equal partner in ministry, values my opinions and loves leading with me. Upon moving into the Edgewater neighborhood of Chicago we quickly realized how important it was for me to have the title "pastor." We noticed an interesting thing happens when Rich meets someone new and says he is a pastor. At best people begin confessing the last time they went to church, and at worst the conversation ends. But when I introduce myself as a pastor, at best they visit our church, and at worst they ask for more information about the church. No, titles are not the end all-be all goal for women or men in ministry. In Chicago, however, my title helps lead people to Jesus. Ultimately it's not about titles; it's about calling. As long as I can be obedient to God's calling on my life, I can give or take the title.

So when do I feel anonymous in ministry? Ironically, it's when I attend Christian conferences or other events for church planters and pastors. I am happy to be Rich's wife and I am thrilled to be introduced that way. Meeting and marrying Rich continues to be one of the best parts of my life. At the same time, I can't help but notice how Rich rarely gets introduced as Dori's husband, though I know he'd be just as thrilled with that introduction.

Rather than fight this or face being misunderstood, I tend to adjust in these moments, to think of what Jesus would do and to err on the side of humility. After all, God doesn't seem too bothered by being anonymous in the book of Esther.

But does this anonymity have to continue? As the mother of two girls, I can't help but wonder, "What will life in the church be like for them?" I see Charis and Nia as two incredibly strong people, made in the image of God to reflect the glory of God in the unique ways God has gifted them. In a world where their bodies are often treated as tools and their minds are often seen as threats, what will the church offer them? What will the Bride of Christ give to these girls who may or may not become brides themselves? Whether or not they ever start a church, my hope is that we begin seeing the role of women within the church as vital to the mission of God. Nia and Charis are not anonymous. None of our daughters are.

So I come back to this book in your hands. It was Debbie Jones who also challenged me to put my name on it. Not for fame, not for glory—it is Jesus alone who deserves our praise. No, when Debbie asked me to put my name on this book she validated me as a woman, as a minister, as a mother, as a writer, and as a wife. That's what naming does—it validates the one being named. She also validated the women whose stories fill the pages ahead. Just like there are many characters in Esther, there are many people who are a part of this book—21 to be exact. The bulk of writers who contributed their stories to this book are Bloom church planting women, some with titles and some without, but make no mistake, all significant. In addition to these Bloom church planters, several other women—from different countries, denominations, churches and ministries—have added their stories. It is my hope that this diverse group of often-anonymous women will reveal the handprint of the often-anonymous God. It is my hope that by naming God in the story of Esther, we will find our names in the stories of church planting. It is my hope that all of our names will come together to lift up the Name above all names, Jesus Christ.

So here I am. My name is Dori and I'm sticking with the women.

INTRODUCTION

# CHURCH PLANTING AND THE BOOK OF ESTHER

"I didn't know Esther planted a church." This tongue in cheek response from a former seminary professor makes me smile. These were his words when I told him about this book. Yes, he is correct. Spoiler alert—Esther was not a church planter. It would be challenging to plant the Body of Christ within the Persian Empire approximately 400 years before Christ has even appeared in flesh and blood.[1] While Esther was not a church planter, the book of Esther has at least five themes that connect with the lives of church planting women.

## LIMITED POWER ISN'T ALWAYS BAD[2]

If not a church planter, then who was Esther? She was a young, single woman. She was Jewish and she was an orphan. These five identity-forming words—young, single, woman, Jewish and orphan—handed her a full deck stacked against her. The odds were not in her favor. It is from this position of limited power that Esther's story begins to connect with the lives of church

---

1 The book of Esther was set during the reign of the Persian king Ahasuerus (Xerxes I), ruling form 486 to 465 B.C.E. Most modern scholars, based on archeological and contextual evidence, believe the book of Esther was written sometime between the years 400 and 350 B.C.E., before Greece conquered the Persian Empire in 331 B.C.E.

2 Carol M. Betchel, *Esther*, Interpretation: A Biblical Commentary for Teaching and Preaching (Louisville: John Knox Press, 2002), 11. Betchel introduces the theme of "limited power" that runs throughout the book of Esther as well as the "challenge of living a faithful life in an unfaithful culture."

planting women, and even more so to church planting women of color.[3] When women move to a city, a suburb, or a small town to start a church with a team of people or with our families, we have limited power. But so do our male counterparts. The difference for church planting women is that we know our power is limited from day one. Unfortunately, our culture, often reinforced by our churches, has reminded us of this time and again. But is limited power so bad? After all, that is often the precise time when God shows up.

Before moving to Chicago, a woman said to Rich and I, "You're gonna raise the dead!" I won't lie, we laughed a bit at her charismatic enthusiasm. But we quickly learned that we have a limited power when it comes to raising the dead—both literally and figuratively. Ultimately, "Unless the Lord builds the house, the builders labor in vain" (Psalm 127:1). Church planting has given me the opportunity to see God build a house in seemingly impossible circumstances. I've seen a man's vision restored. I've seen a playground renewed. I've seen significant financial needs met in record time. Each of these moments, and many more like them, represent how God has raised the dead in Chicago. If you ask Omar why he came to our church, he responded, "I was losing my vision. You prayed. I was healed. So I come back." If you ask Qiana about the changes to Swift playground located along "Arson Alley," she says, "I never played here as a kid and now I bring my kids to this playground every week." If you ask my dad about the road trip from Nashville to Chicago during which we were given $26,000 in less than 8-hours, he'd say, "Next time keep driving, who knows how much more God will provide!" "I was blind but now I see"—"All things can be made new again"—"With God nothing is impossible"—these are the truths that church planting has given me. And I can't take credit for any of it. I don't have the power to accomplish any of this on my own.

In story after story in the Bible, we see God moving in powerful ways through the weak, the vulnerable and the broken. The book of Esther is no different. When we realize we cannot accomplish anything on our own, when we realize we must fast and pray, when we realize our weaknesses and

---

3  Linda M. Day, Esther (Nashville: Abingdon Press, 2005), 3. Day argues that Esther is of particular importance "when one is 'other' in more than one way, as is Esther, the orphan/woman/Jew." In this way church planting women of color can relate to Esther in unique ways that their white colleagues cannot fully understand. For the sake of clarity, the term "women of color" includes all women of non-white heritage, often with regard to oppression, systemic racism or racial bias.

limitations are great—that is when God displays divine greatness, that is when God provides much needed strength and that is when God uses the supposed "weak" to humble the perceived "strong." Irony of all ironies, the limited power handed to women by generations of patriarchy has actually created great space for God's glory to be revealed. Don't hear me incorrectly; God does not glory in the mistreatment of women nor does God dictate it. But God does glory in redeeming the marginalized, in providing a place for the outcast, in comforting the neglected and in raising the dead. In the end I can live with limited power in this present world, knowing I have an otherworldly Power that is vital to planting a church.[4]

## THE GUTS AND THE GLORY OF REVERSALS[5]

As God's power works in mighty ways through those with limited power, we see a glimpse of God turning things upside down. There are many of these "reversals" throughout the book of Esther.[6] One banquet ends with the dethroning of a queen (1:9) while another banquet begins with the coronation of a new queen (2:18). Haman is honored by the king (3:1), but then Haman is asked to honor Mordecai on behalf of the king (6:6-10). Ahasuerus and Haman toast their glasses after sealing the decree to annihilate the Hebrew people (3:15), only to later see the Jews feasting and celebrating a new edict in their favor (8:17). The Persian banquets at the beginning of the book (1:2-8) are reversed with the feasts at the end of the book (9:17-19).

Church planting women and men are no strangers to these kinds of reversals. Often what we set out to do in ministry gets turned upside down. How we thought things would be can end up exactly the opposite of what we initially imagined. Friends on our launch team leave us, our "target audience" changes, plans fall through, neighborhoods gentrify, agreements are broken, deaths occur, venues move, no one shows up and the list goes

---

4 I must acknowledge that this living with "limited power in this present world" is much easier for me as a white woman born in the United States. My perspective here definitely reveals my privilege. Other women, similar to Esther, may find this much more challenging and even life-threatening than I do.

5 Jon D. Levenson, *Esther: A Commentary*, The Old Testament Library (Louisville: Westminster John Knox Press, 1997), 8. Levenson quotes Brooks Schramm who argued in a seminar at the University of Chicago Divinity School that "the theme of the entire book is summed up in two Hebrew words—*nahăpōk hū'*, 'the reverse occurred' (9:1)."

6 Betchel, *Esther,* 5-6.

on and on. Ministry is anything but predictable and God cannot be put into a box. Evil is often exalted, good leaders are at times dethroned and spiritual forces are at work to celebrate the downfall of a new church.

While all of these losses are real and must be grieved, we do not grieve as those without hope (1 Thess 4:13). We hold fast to the Lord, hoping that we will see the Spirit of God exalted, the coronation of Jesus in our neighborhoods and the deepening growth of a church that is working fervently to join God's work in the world.[7] After all, the cross was a reversal the disciples were not prepared to face; but so was the resurrection. Unexpected outcomes can be tragic, but they can also be glorious.

IT'S OKAY TO LAUGH

Within all of these reversals, the book of Esther reminds us it is okay to laugh. No, the annihilation of a group of people is no laughing matter. And if the story of Esther were told from the vantage point of a modern day historian, then it would not be funny at all. But Esther is not written in the same way we write history today. The audiences who, years later, heard this story retold at the festival of Purim, were likely not bothered by the facts of the story.[8] They are more likely concerned with the truths of the story—what can be learned from it, how we must savor it and how we can laugh in the midst of it. Esther is filled with "exaggeration, caricature, ludicrous situations, practical jokes, coincidences, improbabilities, and verbal humor."[9]

Church planting women have a unique vantage point when it comes to seeing the ironies, the hilarities, the correlations and even the caricatures in ministry. I've seen people stand up in the middle of a sermon and call out the guest speaker for being a "false prophet." I've heard a group of completely un-churched teenagers misunderstand the chant "Jesus! Jesus! Jesus!" at a youth conference. We only discovered the mistake when one

---

7 Blackaby, Henry. *Experiencing God.* (Nashville: B&H Publishing, 2008), 56. From "Reality Three: God invites you to become involved with Him in His work."

8 Modern biblical scholars use various genres to describe the book of Esther, but all share some element of "fictionality." Betchel wisely advises, "In using this term we should be careful not to equate fiction with untruth...Fiction, then, is not the *absence* of truth, but often the *vehicle* for it" (4).

9 Adele Berlin, *Esther,* JPS Bible Commentary (Philadelphia: Jewish Publication Society, 2001), 14.

of the students turned to an adult leader and asked, "Why are we yelling 'Cheezits! Cheezits! Cheezits!'?" I've seen my own daughter terrified of baptism services because of the unexpected and loud clapping and yelling as the baptized person comes out of the water. The irony of the pastors' kid having a near anxiety attack at the mention of a baptism celebration can't be missed.

When church planting women get together we automatically have stories in common. These stories need to be told. I've heard of a church-planting woman who has been baptized over 15 times. No, not because she believes in re-baptism, but simply because someone was nervous about being baptized and needed to see what it looked like—and she has volunteered over 15 times to be the "example." I've heard stories of crazy church softball leagues, misprinted signs, preaching mishaps and more. We all need safe spaces to vent, to be heard and to laugh until we cry. You will read some of these stories in the pages ahead; I invite you to laugh with us. Sometimes it's a different kind of laughter. If you listen closely enough, you may hear us laughing so as not to cry. Both the laughter and the tears are necessary as our stories are told.

## THE POWER OF STORIES

In the movie *The Shadowlands*, C.S. Lewis' character says, "We read to know we're not alone."[10] Just like the book of Esther and the world of church planting often create laughable experiences, both share similarities when it comes to the significance of the written word.[11] As mentioned earlier, the story of Esther is now retold annually at the festival of Purim. Within the story itself, we see the significance of the written word being retold to King Ahasuerus one night as he struggles with insomnia (Esther 6). The written record of Mordecai saving the king actually becomes the instrument by which the king saves Mordecai.[12]

I have always been a writer. Not for the purpose of publishing but for my own mental, emotional and spiritual health. I have kept some kind of journal since I was in middle school. Of course I have seasons when I

---

10  *Shadowlands*, prod. and dir. Richard Attenborough, 132 minutes, Price Entertainment, 1993, DVD.

11  Betchel, *Esther*, 15-16.

12  _____, 15.

am more faithful and seasons when I'm lucky to get a paragraph down on paper. But no matter the season, putting pen and paper to my thoughts and prayers has helped me in indescribable ways. I have noticed that since starting a church six years ago, my journaling has taken on a different form. I'm not as guarded in what I say. I've stopped caring who may one day read these journals. I've started getting very honest with God and with myself. Writing, reading and re-reading my journals has provided much-needed perspective for me as a church planting woman.

Writing your story for others to read is a vulnerable, powerful endeavor. Attempting to articulate what Jesus is doing in and through our personal stories is not for the faint at heart. Reading the stories of others is also significant. You can find a sense of familiarity as you read of a shared experience, or you can gain wisdom as you uncover your own inexperience. Something happens in you as you write and something has the potential to happen within you as you read. The women who have written their stories within these pages are strong, intelligent and bold individuals. While their stories are uniquely significant, they each agree that they are not center stage.

## WHO IS THE MAIN CHARACTER?

Many have argued over the true hero of the book of Esther. For decades scholars exalted Mordecai as the unsung hero, directing Esther's every move.[13] Others have pointed out that it was Mordecai who got the Jewish people in a mess to begin with, leaving it up to Esther to step in and save the day.[14] What if both perspectives are correct and at the same time both are completely wrong? God is the main character of Esther, just like God is the main character of the entire Bible. Both Esther and Mordecai play significant roles, joining with God to bring hope to the people of God. But God is center stage.

What do we do with a God who is at the center yet remains unnamed throughout the entire book of Esther? Readers are forced to discern God's handprint in the coincidences, in the prayers, in the "other quarters" (4:14)

---

13   Betchel, 10.

14   _____.

found throughout the book. Isn't this just like our lives, and specifically the lives of church planting women? Often we do not get a word from God to uproot our lives and move to a certain city or town. Often we do not have a prophetic vision telling us what we must say and what we must do to best serve the people and place God has called us. We are at times responsible for making decisions that may have serious consequences for others, for our families and for ourselves. On many occasions we cannot see how our stories will end as we are living in the "frightening middle."[15] Interestingly, some of Jesus' last words were, "And surely I am with you always, to the very end of the age" (Matthew 28:19-20), but then he leaves.[16] His bodily form departs from this earth, leaving us with an often-unnamed God to guide us.

## SUMMARY

It is through the power of the Holy Spirit that we, as church planting women, grow in faith. By faith we must believe that our limited power can be redeemed for God's glory. By faith we must trust that goodness can come in the midst of gut-wrenching reversals. By faith we somehow manage to laugh in the midst of life-altering circumstances. By faith we risk putting our stories on paper to join with the stories of Vashti, Esther, Mordecai, Haman and Ahasuerus. By faith we hear the words "for such a time as this" and somehow find the courage to say, "If I perish, I perish." By faith we name this unseen God as Jesus. By faith we walk to the edge of darkness and take one more step.[17] We are church planting women. We play a role in the story, alongside church planting men. Both women and men are significant. At the same time, neither a man nor a woman is the main character. It is God who is center stage. It is God who gets the glory. It is God who must be named and who does the naming. It is God whose handprint is all over the stories of Esther as well as these stories of church planting women. May you name God in these pages and may God name you through our stories.

---

15   Karen H. Jobes, *The NIV Application Commentary* (Grand Rapids: Zondervan Publishing House, 1999), 48.

16   _____, 49.

17   This is how my childhood pastor defined faith. Rick White often said, "Faith is walking to the edge of darkness and taking one more step."

ANONYMOUS

CHAPTER ONE

# VASHTI
## JUST SAY NO

"I love your voice." "Are you a boy?" "You could be on the radio." "You sound so sultry." "Your voice doesn't annoy me like most female speakers." I have grown up with many people making comments like these, and more, about my voice. If you were able to hear me speak right now you would likely make a similar observation. I live with a unique voice; but so does everyone. The question is, how do we use our unique voices?

The voice of Vashti is unique as well. Ironically, we never actually hear Vashti's voice in the book of Esther. She is spoken to and she speaks through the king's attendants, a group of seven eunuchs. Her story is then told through a narrator whose clear focus is on King Ahasuerus and a conversation he has about Vashti with a group of legal advisors. The name "Vashti" is simply placed within a story that is within a book that is named Esther, the queen who replaced Vashti on the throne. So how do we hear Vashti's voice when it is clear the author of Esther chose not to reveal much about her?[1] Let's begin with the words we have:

> Esther 1, NRSV
> *⁵When these days were completed, the king gave for all the people present in the citadel of Susa, both great and small, a banquet lasting for seven days, in the court of the garden of the king's palace... ⁹Furthermore, Queen Vashti gave a banquet for the women in the palace of King Ahasuerus. ¹⁰On the seventh day, when the king was*

---

1 Betchel, *Esther*, 24 and Day, *The NIV Application Commentary*, 30.

*merry with wine, he commanded Mehuman, Biztha, Harbona, Bigtha and Abagtha, Zethar and Carkas, the seven eunuchs who attended him, [11]to bring Queen Vashti before the king, wearing the royal crown, in order to show the peoples and the officials her beauty; for she was fair to behold. [12]But Queen Vashti refused to come at the king's command conveyed by the eunuchs. At this the king was enraged, and his anger burned within him.*

Before we ever hear her voice, we read her name. Vashti is a Persian name, which shares similarities with an Arabic noun meaning 'Beautiful One' or as a name 'Beautiful Woman.'[2] Both Ahasuerus and the 'Beautiful Woman' Vashti are in the middle of hosting their own banquets, presumably with their own genders,[3] when a message is sent to the queen. The king commands her to appear before him and his guests wearing the royal crown. The king's motives are clear—he wants to show off her beauty to his officials and the other men of the palace. Vashti, however, does the unthinkable. She refuses to appear. We do not know her exact words, we do not hear her unique voice in this moment and we do not know her precise motives. All of this is left to the imagination, leaving a large gap for readers to fill.[4]

Jewish rabbis and some modern preachers have filled this gap by warning of the consequences of a rebellious wife. Contrasting Vashti with Esther, Martin Luther encouraged men to "…take an Esther and let Vashti go, as King Ahasuerus did."[5] Contemporary feminist scholars have taken the opposite approach uplifting Vashti as the true heroine of the book "for standing up to the king and refusing to be treated as a sex object, something Esther is accused of failing to do."[6] Although the text itself does contrast Esther with Vashti (Esther 2:17) we must recognize that whether we like it or not, this is not the main point of the book. The writer of Esther is clearly more concerned with King Ahasuerus and the ethnic and racial tensions at play between the Persians and the Jewish people, rather than the tensions between genders. In other words, there is a larger story at work here.

---

2  Abarim Publications, "The Name Vashti in the Bible," http://www.abarim-publications.com/Meaning/Vashti.html (July 27, 2016).

3  Betchel, *Esther*, 23.

4  Day, *Esther*, 30.

5  Walther I. Brandt, ed., *Luther's Works: The Christian in Society*, vol. 45 (Philadelphia: Muhlenberg, 1962), 33-34.

6  Jobe, *The NIV Application Commentary*, 70.

It is this larger story that may help us figure out the different responses of Vashti and Esther when it comes to appearing before the king. Vashti says a clear "No!" to the king. Why did she do this? We can't know for certain. But we do know that Vashti is Persian, and from this perspective she has a heritage, a position, and a privilege of being able to say no. While her gender puts her at a disadvantage, her race, social status and wealth place the possibility of defiance within her grasp.

Personally, I hate that Vashti has often been criticized within the church. We all—men and women alike—need elements of Vashti within us. There are moments when we need to say an uncompromising "No!" regardless of the consequences. There are times when we need to defend ourselves, stand up for an injustice and use our voice. But I am also bothered by the exaltation of Vashti at the expense of Esther. We cannot ignore the fact that Vashti's "No!" was emboldened by her race and status. Her privilege allowed her to quickly respond to the king in defense of her dignity, without fearing the consequences. Yes, Vashti is to be admired, but not at Esther's expense.

What does Vashti's "No!" have to do with church planting women? We all have Vashti stories: times when we have used our voices in bold ways; times when we have taken a stand against an injustice; times we have discovered an inner strength we didn't know we had. The lesson of Vashti reminds us, "Be strong and courageous. Do not be afraid or terrified because of them, for the Lord your God goes with you; he will never leave you nor forsake you" (Deuteronomy 31:6). Some of us have done this from the privileged perspective of our dominant race, social status and economic position. Others of us have not had that luxury, and yet we have still walked in the steps of Vashti. The following stories portray our Vashti moments—these are the "No's" of the 'Beautiful Ones' who start, serve and sacrifice so much for the sake of the Gospel.

## JAN LIMIERO

Jan Limiero is an adventurer who loves exploring new areas. Besides rock climbing and backpacking, the biggest adventure she has undertaken is church planting. Jan and her husband David started Life Journey Church (lifejourneychurch.com) in Bakersfield, CA. They have three kids, two of whom have been released into the Wild. She is a life coach and spiritual director and serves on the leadership team of Bloom, Stadia's ministry for church planting women. She has a passion for guiding people, especially those in ministry, to a greater connection with God and His Kingdom.

## THE HIGH COST OF SAYING NO

I underestimated the battleground that church planting incites. In our previous ministry in Illinois, I had been our Small Groups Director and was responsible for quadrupling the number of our groups, implementing coaching huddles for our leaders and seeing many people grow in discipleship because of their healthy group relationships and studies. How hard could it be to start over and do the same thing from the ground up in our new church plant in California?

Even before we launched the public worship services for our new church, we started several small groups in the community. Everyone on our leadership team was encouraged to be in a group, if not lead a group. Everything was lining up neatly until one team leader informed me their group would have to be closed to any new people. Instead of allowing their group to grow and multiply into other groups, they valued bonding as friends and felt it best not to have new people coming into this budding trust relationship. While that might be well and good in an existing church with plenty of group options, we were in the critical stage of inviting people into our larger blossoming community. We needed many places for people to establish relationships. This tight group of our leaders was closing the door to that need. So I said "No."

The leader, however, was not asking for my approval. He was informing me of their decision, which made my "No" a bit shocking to his resolute decision. I met with the leader and explained our values and the need to have open groups at this stage of our church plant, but it did no good. He did not see my perspective and locked his knees hard, protecting his stance. He didn't see how I could "dictate" who could be in his group by telling him his group needed to be open to more than just his current Christian, churched friends.

I have rarely, if ever, had anyone oppose my ministry leadership like this. Sensing that more than a little of this issue could have to do with gender roles, I cautiously employed my husband, the pastor, to intervene and speak for "the church," not just my position.

Unfortunately, that was like throwing a mouse into the middle of a catfight! The sequence of events that followed is now a welcome blur. Several shocking and demoralizing meetings later, my husband and I were both accused of being dictators. Rumors started to spread throughout our leadership team and all the way back to our home church in Illinois. This leader now declared he was sent by God to watch over us and keep us in line, single-handedly ensuring the success of our church. An icy chill seemed to sweep by us like an invisible wraith. What was happening?

Like Vashti, sticking to our values with this one "No" cost us a high price. She eventually lost her throne; ours was shaken. Not only did gossip cause others to question our reputation out here in the Wild West, but we also began to question our decisions. Should we have let him do what he wanted and just ignore this rogue group? Was it worth it? Maybe we were dictators. Self-doubt is a shaky foundation for leaders and will cost you sorely.

That entire small group left the church, taking their family and friends from other groups with them. Whole families leaving also means money leaving at a time when finances were critical to getting this fledgling church off the ground. This seemingly small "No" rippled into what I now affectionately call "The Exodus" in our church history. We quickly lost more than 30 percent of our church just after its first year of existence, leaving the rest of our crowd to question our leadership ability.

The pruning of a rose bush is shocking to look at initially, however, it eventually brings healthy new growth. Over time our church actually grew to be healthier than before. The loss turned into gain as our values were instilled and embraced by a tighter leadership team. Doubt turned into steadfastness based on what God was speaking to us.

We heard God's voice and followed those directions regardless of approval from others. Instead of "fear of man" and people pleasing, our trust in God's goodness, regardless of appearances, grew profoundly deep roots. That next year we baptized three times the number of people as in our first year, and our numbers slowly grew back with people who were in harmony with our vision and values.

Little did I know that the voice boldly established in me during those early years would bear fruit years later in a different scenario where I timidly agreed to give the Sunday message. I couldn't quite bring myself to call it preaching, based in part on my "Bible Belt" upbringing where that would not be right for a woman. At the same time, I knew God burned a message in me for our church to hear.

We had a congregation of people with varied backgrounds, including some who openly opposed women in leadership, much less the pulpit. I knew that sticking to what God was calling me to do would inevitably bring condemnation from a small few. Of that small few, the ones who mattered the most to me were our only missionaries, a couple who had come home from the mission field wounded, yet had found a safe place to heal in our church.

We had slowly placed them into our core leadership and eventually sent them back out to the mission field. He announced flatly that he would cut off our partnership and refuse our mission support if I took the pulpit on a Sunday. But trusting his heart over his dogma, we again said "No."

My husband had a lovingly gentle video call with him to listen to his concerns and assure him we would still send financial support whether he agreed with our choice or not.

The outcome of this episode, unlike the last, was uneventful. I spoke on that Sunday, the relationship persevered, support was sustained and later on we visited this family overseas as the friendship continued. That first "No" and the long-lasting effects, both positive and negative, was fertilizer for our ministry and also for my formation. I learned the spiritual value of a well-placed "No."

As Vashti learned, a "No" can be like the explosion of a bomb. Under the direction of God's voice, however, it can also be the flick of a domino starting a chain reaction that leads to the good of those called according to His purpose (Romans 8:28).

## SARA MCGUE

Sara McGue is a storyteller, educator, speaker and writer who loves to lead others to find their "true identity" in Christ. She has authored and co-edited *Bloom Where You Are Planted Vol. III.* Sara is a champion for reconciliation among all people. She and her husband Matt first founded LifePointe Christian Church (lifepointecc.com) in Charlotte, North Carolina in 2004 and then ONE Church (thatonechurch.org) in Jackson, Mississippi in 2014. Both churches are multi-ethnic, gospel-centered, difference-making, healthy church plants with the support of Stadia. Sara and Matt have two grown children, Mikel and Benjamin. Sara loves being "MiMi" to her two grandchildren, Grayson and Naomi. Presently, Sara has the privilege of leading Bloom's Special Projects Team.

## SAYING NO CAN MEAN SAYING YES

This is her place of refuge where she finds her inner peace. On the balcony just off her quarters she doesn't have to be the Queen of Persia, but simply Vashti. As she closes her eyes and breathes in deeply she can smell the fragrances that are being placed in her bath to prepare for the banquet tonight. She also smells the home fires being stoked to prepare dinners across the kingdom. The late afternoon sun warms her arms and the specks of sand stroke her face in the breeze as she hears the branches of the palms below rustling in the wind.

These are the moments she cherishes, all to herself, without her attendants fluttering around. She sometimes can't believe she is the Queen of Persia with her husband Ahasuerus as the most powerful man in the world. There is a storm blowing in and as she stands on the roof overlooking the kingdom of Persia, she can't help but have a foreboding in her spirit.

The scriptures are unclear when it comes to the destiny of Vashti. By saying "No" to the king, there were two possible consequences, either death or exile. I can't help but wonder what it was like for Vashti to escape death only to live out the rest of her life in exile. Her fate would be written in the scriptures and history books as the woman who said "No" to her king! Although she stood up against exploitation at the hand of her husband, I wonder what became of her legacy? What stories of Vashti remain untold?

Fast-forward 2,500 years and today, like Vashti, women are still fighting the stereotypes that have been passed down for generations. I prefer to view Vashti as a heroine of the story of Esther because I can hear her voice moving beyond Persia to impact the church today. Many of us today are embroiled in the "tug of war" between saying no for the sake of the kingdom of God or yes for the sake of another, lesser kingdom.

I am writing this in the early hours of the morning, where I can shut things off and just "rest in the Lord." After planting two multi-ethnic, multi-cultural churches, the last 13 years have taught me multiple times how to say "No." My husband and I have a passion for planting churches that look like heaven and strive to act like heaven on earth. Our church in Jackson is unique because it is the first church since the founding of the state in 1817 to ever start with one African-American pastor and one White pastor, serving alongside of each other as co-pastors. 200 years later and we are still fighting the battles of segregation in Mississippi.

When praying over this chapter about Vashti, the Lord laid on my heart such a burden for unity and reconciliation. These are issues that keep me up at night with the weight of the lost who have yet to meet Jesus! My "No" story was more of an internal struggle, the one of being comfortable with the status quo.

I am a Southern girl, born and raised in the South, but raised in a household that did not discriminate, period. I was raised in a military house, my father was a commanding officer and I was the youngest of five. I always had friends of different ethnicities and races. With this background, it wasn't until I was 48 years old that I had to face, head-on, the stigma of 'white privilege.' Those words together make my stomach turn, but now that I live in the 'Deep South' this is an everyday reality even though it is 2017.

I had to examine my own heart to see the impact of "white privilege" within me. I never believed I was allowed into doors simply by the color of my skin, but it was true. I now had to decide how I was going to use my privilege to get others in the door, that otherwise would have never been invited, to challenge subjects from educational reform to segregation in Mississippi. I learned to say, "No, I will not stand for the status quo. I will work to fight against systemic racism." I have to say "No" in order to help bring about the changes that are so desperately needed in my community, my city, my state and in our country.

I am passionate about early childhood education. My work as an educational consultant allowed me to witness first-hand the oppression in our state. I saw buildings crumbling with out of date textbooks in some schools, while other schools stockpiled resources in the corners of classrooms. Many times I would come home with a heavy heart and tell my husband, "I feel as if I stepped back in time to the 1960s." It was evident that the "black schools" were not taken care of as they should have been, with the leftovers being sent to them. I was, however, able to meet and work with educators who, out of love for their students and their profession, keep moving along. These women and men are the unsung heroes to me, as they endure such difficult situations yet keep on teaching for 185 days of the year. It is these teachers who say, "No, I will not give up. I will continue to educate my students despite the circumstances."

These are the experiences that have left an indelible mark in my spirit as I have chosen to fight for these children and educators. Today society throws around the saying 'the children are our future,' yet the same society shackles children to a dismal future. While "the elephant in the room" is obvious, it is rarely addressed. In Mississippi and our country, we have to be willing to stand up and say "No" to the injustices that have been brought against those who don't look like me, talk like me or vote like me.

My mother would often tell me, "Sara, you have a keen sense of justice around you—allow it to embolden you and fight for those who can't!" So in my way, I am saying "No" to the status quo by using my 'white privilege' to open doors that have been shut for decades. I will continue to be a conduit for change, whether that is slowly opening the door or kicking it in.

Just like Vashti, saying "No" to the kings of this world enables you to say "Yes" to something else. We will never know Vashti's fate. No historian has ever written about the rest of her life, so it is left to our imagination. I choose to think that Vashti watched from afar as this new Queen Esther would change the fate of a nation in a different way. Vashti's "No" brought Esther's "Yes" and the world of the Hebrew people was forever changed.

**VANESSA PUGH**

Vanessa Pugh is passionate about empowering women to grow in their leadership. She is a fierce lover of people; few things bring her joy like watching those around her succeed. In 2009, Vanessa and her husband Scott planted Velocity Church (velocitycleveland.org) in Cleveland, Ohio in partnership with Stadia. As a key leader at Velocity, Vanessa leads small groups, creates ministry teams, recruits volunteers, trains leaders and preaches on Sundays. She is the Assistant Director of Bloom, a ministry of Stadia that exists to empower women to maximize their role in starting churches. Vanessa enjoys coaching softball, reading autobiographies and is the Cleveland Cavaliers unofficial team Mom.

## MORE THAN A LABEL

I had never known a pastor's wife before. Having never gone to church growing up, I didn't even know the label existed. Little did I know I would one day become a 'pastor's wife.'

I grew up in a little pocket of Akron, Ohio called North Hill. It was an incredible place to grow up. To this day, you can still get some of the most delicious Italian food you've ever tasted in North Hill. In many ways North Hill was a typical blue collar suburb. Yet the folks who call North Hill home seem to be made of tougher material than most. This is where I learned to stand up for myself and to persevere. This is where I bled and cried, discovering I was stronger than I thought. I've always been proud of my North Hill roots.

The one thing, however, I never came across in 'The Hill' as a pastor's wife. Out of my group of childhood friends, most of them never went to church. For those who did, our religious differences were never an issue. "You be you"—that's just how it was. Although I have many wonderful childhood memories, I have an equal amount of regret. I spent a large part of my life with excellent manners but no morals. The decisions I made led me to become someone I never knew I could be. My childhood and adolescent years can be summed up in a few words. Athlete. Popular. Bully.

At the end of my freshman year of college, I found myself firmly planted at rock bottom. I decided to drop out of school and get a full-time job. It was during this brief season of my life when I met Jesus. An older couple I had known in high school had recently become Christians and they reached out to me, excited to share the gospel with me. I had never in my life heard this good news they shared with me.

I lived the first 19 years of my life without knowing there was a God who loved me, a God who died for me, a God who desired a relationship with me and a God who had a plan for my life. But on that day, sitting with that couple in an Outback Steakhouse, I came to believe in Jesus and professed him as my Savior. I had no idea that my life was starting on a path I had never dreamed.

It wasn't long after I became a Christian that news of my newfound religion made its way around North Hill. I spent the next several months trying to purge my life of many of the things that had taken me to rock bottom. I never judged the people I left behind. I knew, however, if I didn't get away from it all, then my new attempt at a better life would be short lived. It wasn't easy. I had never been an outcast. My whole life I had been popular, so it was a very lonely season. I learned that saying "No" can cost you a lot. I also learned that sometimes the cost of saying "No" is worth it.

About six months after giving my life to Jesus, I met a boy. Scott was unlike anyone I'd ever met before. He was friendly, outgoing, funny and had a very magnetic personality. Truthfully, he was the first Christian guy I'd ever met. We spent a lot of time together, but our relationship was strictly platonic. Over time I learned that Scott used to be a pastor. At the time, however, he was working for his family business while finishing a Master in Communications.

It didn't take long for us to realize we liked each other and wanted to be more than just friends. It was 15 months between our first kiss and our wedding day. Once we were married, we decided it was time to find a church to call home. We found a great little church around the corner from our house and enjoyed the first couple years of marriage attending there and volunteering with the youth ministry.

Two years after we were married, Scott felt an unyielding call on his life to return to full-time ministry. Within a few weeks he had multiple job offers from different churches, and he had never even sent out a resume. He accepted a position at the church we were currently attending and at the age of twenty-two I stepped into a new role too. I was now a 'pastor's wife' and I still had no idea what that meant.

As a 'pastor's wife' what was I supposed to say "Yes" to and when should I say "No"? I had no clue. The other pastor's wives at that church, unfortunately, were not very helpful. From them I mostly learned that pastor's wives were rigid, unapproachable and prone to gossip. In spite of this, the people of the church still held them in a high regard. I have since learned that not all pastor's wives from traditional churches are like this. But during that time of my life, these first examples were all I had.

Another intense call from God came into Scott's life seven years later. Church planting—something neither of us knew much about. While I trusted Scott and knew I would support him completely, I was also terrified about what this would mean for me. In the early phases of our church plant I was forced to wrestle with my identity as the 'pastor's wife.' On one hand, I had the traditional pastors' wives from our last church. But they were an enigma to me as people placed them on a pedestal even though they never did much to contribute. On the other hand, I had the super-trendy, uber-talented, Starbucks-loving church planting wives I had most recently encountered and admired. I was torn between the traditional and the trendy—I couldn't find my place. Neither seemed to fit me. In some ways, like Vashti, I was being called to stand before the church to present myself, but I didn't know who I was supposed to be.

I began to deeply resent the pressure of the 'pastor's wife' label. As we pursued church planting I experienced emotional shut-down on so many levels. I missed the people and relationships from my past and found it emotionally draining to start new ones. It was hard to read my Bible or talk to God. I felt so inadequate in this new endeavor and still couldn't figure out what my role was supposed to be as the 'pastor's wife.' As a result, I left myself wide open to spiritual attack. In the 14 years Scott and I have now been in ministry, I have never experienced such warfare. The more I retreated into myself, the worse it got. I didn't tell Scott what was going on because I didn't want him to be discouraged. So for about six months, the enemy had his way with me. I was angry all the time and had a volatile temper. I refused to read or pray, and I secretly hoped our mission would fail so I wouldn't have to face the reality that I felt completely inadequate without a purpose. It was such a dark and scary time for me.

After several months, I finally cracked. Scott and I were driving in the car and he could feel the negativity radiating from me. In a very exasperated tone he asked, "What is wrong with you?!" At that moment I broke down. Through my tears, I poured my heart out and told him everything. I told him my fears, my anger and how I felt the enemy oppressing me with such immense force. I felt so ashamed for letting this happen to me. I know what Scripture says, I know how powerful the devil is, and I know God is much more powerful. In this season, however, I had forgotten. Scott immediately pulled the car over, put his hands on my shoulders and started to pray. I continued to cry as he prayed. I can't explain it, but it felt as if the Devil was loosening his grip as Scott was praying. In that moment Scott helped me say "No" to Satan. When we finished praying I had an immediate sense of release.

The next morning I got up early, made a cup of coffee and, for the first time in a very long time, opened my Bible to begin to study. I spent a long time talking to God and an even longer time listening. It felt so good to be getting back into this rhythm.

When I finally realized what had happened I was overwhelmed with emotion and felt a strong sense of resolve within me. I began to discover that the enemy had a two-fold plan from the start—to come after Scott and to come after me. Satan knew that breaking me would be the best way to get to Scott. Satan also came after me with such tenacity because he knew the impact I could make if I lived into my identity in Christ. But God had no intention of letting me sit this one out. God did not want me to hide behind the scenes, offering little parts of myself to our church plant. God had big plans for me and I almost missed it!

God wants to use my gifts, my life experiences and my lack of a church background to reach the unreachable. When I finally realized it, my inner North Hill rose up, and I told Satan, "No! You are messing with the wrong girl!" Suddenly I had such clarity about the label of 'pastor's wife.' At that moment I refused to back down. I decided no one has the right to define the label 'pastors' wives.' No one has the right to place expectations on us and tell us who we should be. I don't have to fit into any stereotype this world has created. Not one. My responsibility is to look at the gifts, experiences, and personality God has given me and use them for the glory of God. That's it.

So I said to Satan, "No! The 'pastor's wife' will not be moving to Cleveland to plant Velocity Church, but Vanessa will be." When God has a task for me, no matter how intimidating, unorthodox or uncomfortable it may be, I will say "Yes" to Jesus. Since then there have been plenty of things God has called me to do, from leading small groups, to creating teams, to recruiting volunteers, to training leaders and to preaching. I don't have to be anyone other than who God created me to be. I don't have to do anything other than what God asks me to do.

Being bold enough to church plant with that mindset has inspired other women at Velocity to lead and serve where they are gifted and passionate, even if it's not where culture dictates. I have had the privilege of working with many other women who feel trapped in the tension of the 'pastor's wife' label. These women know deep down they are capable of things no one expects. I've watched them rise above the label and become powerhouse servants for the Kingdom. This has been one of the most incredible things I've experienced during the church planting journey.

I encourage women to show up, be seen and serve with all the power and talent God has given you. As the late columnist Erma Bombeck wrote, "When I stand before God at the end of my life, I would hope that I would not have a single bit of talent left, and could say, 'I used everything you gave me.'"

We are so much more than the label 'pastor's wife' implies. We are women in the church and we're using everything God has given us.

## JACQUELINE ARELLANO

Jacqueline Arellano is the First Impressions Director and Global Ministry Advocate at the Aurora Campus of Community Christian Church (communitychristian.org/aurora). Knowing we all hurt as we seek love and acceptance in life, Jacqueline enjoys welcoming and serving others with a huge smile and a hug. She's passionate about orphan care and lovingly embracing people as Jesus does. She's a gifted communicator, with the amazing ability to preach bilingually, rotating between Spanish and English. She's happily married to Obe Arellano. They enjoy days with her son, DeVonn, while also awaiting the arrival of their two children from Haiti. She enjoys the outdoors, especially activities near the Fox River in her beloved Aurora community.

# A VASHTI KIND OF CHURCH

When my husband and I got married, we knew God had brought us together to do His work somehow, somewhere. We spent nights and days dreaming and planning and dreaming some more about what ministry together could look like. We dreamed about a place where my mother who speaks limited English, my son who speaks limited Spanish and myself a fully bilingual Spanish and English speaking 2nd generation Hispanic-American could worship in the same room at the same time on a Sunday morning as a family. We looked at models in the Bible like Paul and Timothy. We loved the early church stories in the book of Acts and longed for that with everything in us. So as soon as we got married, we asked God, "Now, what and where?"

The Lord answered with such clarity as God brought together the right people at the right time to plant a bilingual, multi-generational, multi-ethnic church in Aurora—the second largest city in Illinois with a 90% Latino population. Aurora sure isn't La Jolla in San Diego, California. No, it's far from the beautiful beach town I dreamed about on cold winter nights. Aurora, however, is a resilient place. Decades of gang violence, a declining economy and a struggling public school system have given the city a bad reputation. In light of this, Aurora was not necessarily the ideal place to move my already troubled teenage son, who had grown up fatherless and was now learning to live with a new father figure in the house. Our new family took a step of faith, however, and on January 1, 2007 we drove into our new city to shine the light of Jesus on Aurora, the "City of Lights."

We were determined to shine the love of Jesus into the lives of others, hoping to cause a ripple effect of love, joy and peace in a city many had discarded decades before. We prayed for Jesus to be Lord and we joined arms with other pastors who had been working in this city for decades before we arrived. We learned from them and they empowered us to join the fight against all the darkness that had hurt this city. Together we would help it rise from the ashes of gang violence, below average income brackets and a lower quality educational system.

When we first drove into Aurora on that cold January day, little did we know how our stories had prepared us for what we were going to need to plant a church in this city. We both came from immigrant families and had lived in hard neighborhoods, we both struggled with the challenges of growing up as a minority and we were both fully bilingual. As 2nd generation Hispanic-Americans we had learned English as a second language and also learned to navigate life between two cultures. We knew what it was like to fear police officers because of our immigration status. We also knew what it was like to need financial aid at one time or another in our lives. With all of this in our stories, we were just like many of the families in Aurora.

Everything we had grown up experiencing was about to be used for good, for God's glory. Church planting for us was a perfect marriage between what we had grown up knowing as hardships and what we were now living as redemptive, healing work. What we had endured as children would be used for the good of a new generation.

After much thought and prayer we decided to join forces with an incredible group of people, Community Christian Church. They were starting a new campus in a Hispanic concentrated community of East Aurora. We attended one of their events during the Christmas season called The Gift Mart and it blew our minds. We met Kirsten Strand, Director of Community Christian Church's justice ministry called Community 4:12 and we began to learn about the 'hand-up and not a hand-out' mentality of ministry. We quickly discovered that Community 4:12 cared about the dignity of humans and we were determined to learn more. They had a variety of programs in the community that focused on empowering the youth and the parents. Kirsten was determined to stand up to any injustices against immigrants, refugees and the destitute. As I got to know her and her principles, I knew I had finally found my spot in the church.

After three years of learning more about the city and the community we would be worshipping in, we launched our church. Yes, you read that right—three years. Even though we were the same race, same background and even the same country of origin as many who lived in Aurora, it took three years of immersing in this community to prepare us for planting a church. We volunteered for anything we could get our hands on just to be with the people, learn from them and listen to them so that we could hear what God was saying to us. Every community is different—even if they look like you, speak like you and eat like you. Every neighborhood has its unique gifts as well as heartaches. So we learned, immersed, and learned some more. Nine years later we are still learning.

The past years have taught me that we are a Vashti kind of church. We are a church that has stood up and said "No" to the many injustices this world has thrown into our community and into many other communities. We have said "No" to the injustices of immigration inequality, gender inequality, lack of educational equality, gang violence, depression, suicide, fatherlessness, child abuse and so much more.

We have worked to bring homes to the abandoned, to bring quality education to our community and to bring education to the church when it comes to the importance of immigration rights. We've also strived to learn and teach so many different things, such as: why gang violence happens; what causes domestic violence and why it is unacceptable; why depression and mental health is important to discuss and learn about; why mentoring a parent and teaching them to navigate this new world they are living in is vital; why donating to the homeless shelter that already exists is more efficient than trying to start your own ministry; how serving on advisory boards in City Halls or on Boards of Education is loving your neighbor; how serving as a chaplain for the police department gives you a unique perspective and opportunity to go into people's homes to love them in the midst of their pain. These are just some of the ways we say "No" to the injustices in our city.

We have also learned that our role in the greater church is to help educate the larger body of Christ about what it actually means to love our neighbor as ourselves. Whether they look like us or not, whether they have the same immigration status as us or not, whether they are in the same social or educational class as us or not—how we serve is so important. Do we continue doing things the same way or do we need to make some changes? Does the way we serve enable or empower others? Do we help or hurt? Do we give a hand out or a hand up? Are we truly loving others or feeling sorry for them? Are we serving others or patting ourselves on the back, showing off and perpetuating the 'white savior,' and thus white supremacy, mindset? These are all questions we as a community of God-fearing, Jesus-following, carriers of Light should be asking.

The past nine years have been a rollercoaster. I have learned, cried and had my heart broken one too many times. Through it all, however, these church planting years have been filled with real stories of life change, of people finding their way back to God, their worth and their purpose. My husband and I have sat in messes, in weddings, in graduations and in funerals with our community. When we first drove into Aurora that one January day, we had no clue what we were getting ourselves into. Through it all we commit to keep standing up for people as Jesus would stand, saying "No" to injustice as Vashti did.

CHAPTER TWO

# ESTHER
## BETWEEN SNAKES AND DOVES

*I am sending you out like sheep among wolves. Therefore be as shrewd as snakes and as innocent as doves.*
— Matthew 10:16

My husband Rich says he fell in love with me on a mission trip to India. It was on this trip that our team helped lead a 2,000+ youth conference. And it was at this youth conference where our mission team was asked to commence with the opening ceremony. And it was this precise opening ceremony where we were each given a dove to release into the air. Unfortunately, they didn't have enough doves for everyone so I opted out of holding one. It seemed like the Christian thing to do. It also seemed like the wise thing to do since I absolutely hate birds. I know they are small, but when you have been bitten by a seagull and goosed by a goose (yes, that means what it sounds like), you do not volunteer to hold a dove. Problem solved and crisis averted, right? Not quite. For some unknown reason the people who planned the opening ceremony had the idea of setting off fireworks at the same time we released the doves. Think about that for a minute. Fly away birds, flap your wings and soar high into the deep blue...BOOM! BANG! AHHHH!!! That last scream was mine as a multitude of doves came dive-bombing back to the ground and all I could do was grab the closest person next to me to use as a shield. Thank you, Rich. Did I mention he said he fell in love with me on a mission trip to India? Perhaps that moment should have convinced him otherwise.

Why all this talk about birds? I figured it was best for me to confess my fear of all things fowl before talking about the innocence of a dove. Between snakes and doves—that's where the writer of Matthew asks us to be as we are sent out into this world. Sure, I'm also not a fan of snakes but that's more common. Rare are those of us who hate birds of peace. Nonetheless, we are challenged to be as wise, shrewd and prudent as a snake while at the same time being as innocent and harmless as a dove. Or better said, as innocent as a dove in a painting because in real life they can dive-bomb you!

More than any other person in the Bible, Esther is the epitome of Matthew 10:16. Somehow she manages to be crafty without being deceitful, to be seductive without being manipulative, to be clever without being smarmy. I want to be more like Esther and we need more church planters like her. As a young orphan girl entering the Persian palace, Esther is clearly a sheep among wolves. Esther 2:2-4 tells us the plan for Esther:

> [2]*Then the king's personal attendants proposed, "Let a search be made for beautiful young virgins for the king. [3]Let the king appoint commissioners in every province of his realm to bring all these beautiful young women into the harem at the citadel of Susa. Let them be placed under the care of Hegai, the king's eunuch, who is in charge of the women; and let beauty treatments be given to them. [4]Then let the young woman who pleases the king be queen instead of Vashti." This advice appealed to the king, and he followed it.*

Esther is vulnerable to her own ignorance and inexperience with the ways of the palace. Could the king's eunuch Hegai be trusted? What about the other advisors around the king—wasn't one of them responsible for the banishment of Vashti? Who were the palace sheep that could help Esther and who were the royal wolves in sheep's clothing? The youthful Esther had a lot to learn in a little amount of time. As an orphan, one of the most destitute types of persons in ancient society,[1] Esther would also be an easy target for ridicule among the other women in the king's harem. This wasn't a 'day at the spa with the girls.' While friendships likely formed among them there was no hiding the fact that they were competition. No matter how luxurious their accommodations within the palace, it was no substitute for the security of home and the familiarity of family.[2] This also

---

1 Day, *Esther*, 46.

2 Betchel, *Esther*, 31.

wasn't a modern day beauty contest in which the contestants choose to participate, can go home when it is over and have the chance of receiving some sort of scholarship.[3] The only prize that awaited the king's harem was the prospect of becoming queen—a role that can end just as quickly as it begins, as Vashti reminds us.

Esther also has a secret that puts her at a disadvantage—she is Jewish. Her Jewish name Hadassah is only used once in the book (2:7). Hadassah means myrtle, a sweet scented flower blossom, while Esther means star.[4] Giving a foretaste of what is to come, the Hebrew 'flower' Hadassah is overshadowed by the Persian 'star' Esther. While both are beautiful names with attractive meanings, one shines brighter, eclipsing the other.[5] Hadassah is made anonymous as the young Esther conceals her true identity for the sake of her future. Ironically this future rests on the king remembering the name 'Esther' more than the names of the other young virgins.[6] The king must remember her if she hopes to have a significant future, but the king must not really know her if she hopes to stay alive.

While there is no denying Esther's innocence as a young Jewish orphan girl, there is also no hiding her wisdom. Esther consistently makes wise, thoughtful decisions as she matures in the palace. The young Esther in chapter two who wisely follows the advice of Mordecai and Hegai grows into the Esther of chapter four who now gives advice to Mordecai, asking him to fast as she makes a plan to approach the king despite the risk of death.[7] In chapters five and seven we see Esther become every inch the Queen. She is thorough in her planning of each banquet. She is careful in her wording of each conversation. She is patient in her timing to reveal her true identity. And in the end, she is incredibly persuasive, saving herself as well as rescuing the entire Jewish population. Esther works subversively within the palace system to achieve her desires. She utilizes relational influence rather than positional power to bring about change.[8] While her approach and her demeanor are different, Esther proves equal to Mordecai

---

3  Betchel, 31.

4  Day, *Esther,* 48

5  _____, 46.

6  _____, 52.

7  Betchel, *Esther,* 48.

8  Day, *Esther,* 100.

and the King. Whether you call her Hadassah or call her Esther, there is no doubting her name is Queen.

Six years into our church plant there are many lessons I have learned from Esther. While Vashti encourages me to be bold, to lean in and to speak up, Esther reminds me to be patient, to think first and to earn the right to be heard. Whether in a meeting with the Alderman and the Chief of Police or hanging out with a group of parents after we drop off our kids at school, so much of ministry is about listening, learning and being interested, rather than always trying to be interesting. Distinguishing the "Esther moments" from the "Vashti moments" is especially important when you're starting a new church. You can be banished so easily or you can be welcomed in and trusted. Church planting women live between two worlds—the kingdom of God and the ways of this world. How will we navigate in between these two worlds? How will we live balancing between doves and snakes? This tension is revealed within the following stories of some queenly women who have wisely learned from Esther how to live within their kingdoms.

**LAROSA TATE**

LaRosa Tate is gifted with encouragement and hospitality. She was born in Starkville, Mississippi and graduated with a BA in Industrial Engineering from Mississippi State University. She is married to Albert Tate, the love of her life who is also a gifted communicator and dynamic preacher. After years working as an Industrial Engineer, LaRosa felt called to focus her energies on being at home full-time with her children, Zoe LaRose, Bethany Grace and Isaac Harrison. This also allowed her the opportunity to develop her expertise and passion for mentoring women and serve in a vocal worship ministry. LaRosa and Albert were called by God in 2011 to plant Fellowship Monrovia (madeforfellowship.com), a Stadia partner church in Monrovia, California that is Gospel-centered, multi-ethnic and intergenerational. She currently leads a women's Life Group, serves on the Fellowship Worship Team and co-leads Fellowship Moms, a local moms outreach ministry. In her 'spare' time, LaRosa enjoys reading, traveling with Albert, bargain shopping and date days with her children.

## WHAT HAPPENS IF I DO THIS?

In June 2010 my husband Albert took a retreat. He went away alone to camp and seek God's direction about the future of our ministry and our family. He returned a week later with a vision the Lord had given him to plant a church.

"Wait, what? Why?" Yes, this was my response, coupled with a lot of tears. Why did I respond this way? Well, because this was not a part of the plan. We were comfortable at our church and my kids loved it there. All of our family lived in Mississippi, so our current church in California had become our family. Planting a church would mean uprooting our two beautiful girls from all that was normal to them and leaving behind all of our support. I found myself plagued with fears about what people would think and how they would react.

On top of all that, we had already decided to try for a third child and we needed health benefits. Yes, that was at the top of my list. I questioned what would happen to our benefits? I asked myself would the church be supportive? There were so many questions and so much inner conflict with this new revelation from God for our family. Albert felt it was time for us to go. I did not. I did not initially support this new direction. It took a while for me to be at a place of peace. I imagine Esther was on a journey like mine as Mordecai called her to something she did not expect.

If you're reading this book, then I'm hoping you've also read the story of Queen Esther. One part of this incredible story that sticks out to me is when Mordecai learns the fate of the Jews and tears his clothes, wailing loudly in the city. When Esther learns what Mordecai is doing from her maidens and eunuchs, "the queen writhed in great anguish" and immediately sends clothes to him (Esther 4:4, NASB). Notice her initial reaction. She didn't ask why Mordecai was in sackcloth and ashes, wailing loudly. She wanted to fix things so that he would be comfortable. Esther was comfortable and wanted Mordecai to be comfortable too. She made sure he knew that she saw him. Her response was not sufficient. Mordecai needed Esther to hear his cries and the cries of her people. He needed Esther to see the bigger picture that was happening through her situation.

Esther realized the insufficiency of her response when one of the king's eunuchs, Hathach, returns with a message from Mordecai regarding the fate of the Jews with a copy of the edict. Mordecai was asking Esther to go to the King on behalf of her people. I imagine Esther, like me, may have been a 'rule follower.' Though she understood the seriousness of what Mordecai said, she also knew that going to the King was a serious matter. Esther knew that this could upset everything in her life—her comfort, her 'benefits.' Going before the king uninvited could cost Esther her very life. Mordecai sends Esther another message, reminding her that this was as much about her as it was about all of the Hebrew people. He called her up to what I like to call a "such a time as this" standard. Esther knew Mordecai, but more importantly, she knew the God in Mordecai. His challenge told her she needed to pay attention and act accordingly. And she did.

The thing that changed everything for me was the fact that I loved my husband. I trusted his heart, and the God in him. Because I trusted Albert

I was willing to listen and follow. I would be lying if I told you that I quickly got over my sadness and hopped on the 'let's plant a church' bandwagon. I would follow my husband to the ends of the earth because I trust him that much. This time, however, I followed kicking and screaming.

I cried and prayed a lot. Fortunately, I had many people around me who listened, prayed, and sometimes even cried with me. Albert came home often with news of support and encouragement from church members, leaders and other pastors, yet I could not bring myself to join in his happiness. I was mourning what I would lose when this church plant happened.

Three months after Albert's revelation of our church planting adventure, I wasn't feeling well and stayed home from church. I decided to watch a church service on TV to receive a 'word from the Lord.' I ended up watching two different sermons that day. Both were about stepping out in faith when God calls you, even when it is difficult and doesn't make sense.

When God says go, you go. One of the preachers spoke about Noah and how God called him to do something that didn't make sense. No matter what others said and no matter how ridiculous or uncomfortable it seemed, Noah knew he had to do what God called him to do. That day something awoke inside of me. I finally understood the vision God had given Albert. On that day God gave me something too—peace. When Albert came home from church with excellent news about support for the church plant, for the first time in three months I was able to smile back at him and rejoice with him.

I had been so worried about the reactions of others and the possibility of it not working out that I never stopped to think, "What if we don't answer the call?" Mordecai's second message to Esther pulled her out of saying "What happens to me if I do this?" to saying "What will happen to others if I don't."

One of the many things I appreciate about Albert is his patience. He gave me the space I needed to grieve, pray and find peace. This was not only about trusting Albert. I had to trust God and have confidence that God had called us to plant Fellowship Monrovia "for such a time as this." I had to let go of the 'what ifs,' believing God would provide even when the future was unknown.

Once Esther took that step to approach the King, God's mission was accomplished and the Hebrew people were saved. Esther not only survived her encounter with the King, but she thrived as God continued to give her wisdom for leading as Queen. She would have never known what God could do if she had not taken that bold step. I am so glad Albert and I took that brave step as well. We did not know what the outcome would be. We did not have any idea where we would plant. We did not know if people would come. We did not know if we would have any help. We did not know if we would have any benefits. Yet, God provided. Our church family that we had been a part of for six years prior supported us, loved us, encouraged us and sent us out with their blessing—benefits for a year!

Today, five years since launching the church, our family has grown to three children, which makes our little guy five years old! God has been faithful in ways I never imagined possible. Fellowship Monrovia is a growing and thriving Gospel-centered, multi-ethnic, intergenerational church that exists to make disciples of Jesus Christ. To God be the glory!

**AMANDA PAVICH**

Dr. Amanda Pavich, Ph.D., earned her degree in Biblical Studies from Trinity Theological Seminary in association with the University of Liverpool, England, where she specialized in Biblical Archaeology and Apologetics. A former college professor, she is a trained field archaeologist and a graduate of the International Academy of Apologetics, Evangelism and Human Rights in Strasbourg, France. A passionate advocate for adoption, writer of devotional studies, and teacher of a practical Gospel, she currently serves as the Director of Pastoral Care and Equipping at Grace City Church (gracecitysd.com), launched with Stadia in October 2015 as part of the San Diego Church Plant Movement. She lives mostly outdoors with her family and furry creatures in sunny San Diego, California.

## WARRIOR

*A heart that beats, an Incredible Machine*
*Made of blood and love and hope and lust and steam*
*Calling*
*Calling*
*Calling*

— From "Incredible Machine" by Sugarland (Mercury Records)

If you've ever been at a raw point in your church plant life, exhausted but gaining very little traction, your mind a stagnant pool instead of a tributary for creativity, perhaps you were given this advice: What do you love to do? What is your passion? Follow your heart, do what you love, and you will be successful. You will re-motivate! I agree with the idea of following our passions, but what if we look at it a different way: What makes you angry?

What makes you irrationally emotional? I mean, what makes you really come undone? What about your world makes the warrior within rise to the surface? These angerings can be clues to the heart of God, revealed uniquely in you and me and the churches we launch, that this world desperately needs.

Esther is firstly and most often described as "a woman for such a time as this." What she is revered for is worthy, yes, but perhaps because we are in that long, anonymous stage of a very young church plant, I find myself thinking more about the time before the "time." How much emotional endurance it took. How she experienced early childhood trauma, and then was raised outside the cultural norm as an educated, outspoken Jewess. How she responded upon learning she was being pushed into the palace machine. Her beauty regime was not like going to a relaxing spa day—many of the ancient treatments of 5th century Persia were not very good for you—all the while living within the walls of the do's and don'ts of court culture. She had to hold her tongue and win over her servants, even as she was classified as one object on a shelf of many pretty things. It took strength and perhaps, maybe, a little sass to make it to the "such a time as this."

I find it interesting that the quality of tenacity is still so often perceived as unattractive in women; a man is fighting for what he believes in, a woman is just being a, well, you've heard the word.

Perhaps it is time to re-think that categorization in Christ.

God Himself is tenacious—He relentlessly pursues us, He is swift in His judgment of both sin and righteousness. He is anger and love at the same time. That describes my female heart—the place where anger and love spark and combust to fuel a passionate action.

The opposite of love is not anger, it's apathy. It is not having enough care to warrant action. I define true, biblical love as an unrelenting commitment to doing what is best for another, sometimes having affection for that person, but not always. Otherwise, how could we love our enemies as God asks? How could we walk the fine line of grace? That Esther-grace of honoring those in authority above us, respecting the culture that defines us, while maintaining the heart-muscle strength it takes to know when to speak boldly when we see things done wrongly.

Table-turning tenacity is not like a small child's dogged determination to hold onto what is his. Instead, it is having a mature and teachable understanding of what is right and what is wrong, and then making a commitment to "the good and the right and the lovely." It may involve great personal risk; you may be told the idea won't fly; the outcome may be messy.

It requires clear-headed thinking about the steps we will take, the space we will make, to take action on behalf of those who don't have a voice or don't feel God's love. Passion without a plan is just a dream.

I don't know about you, but I do not want to be known as a dreamer. I want to be known, like Esther, as a warrior.

**DEBBIE JONES**

Debbie Jones is a visionary leader who is passionate about elevating women to discover their unique gifts and how God can use those to have the greatest kingdom impact! She and her husband Tom planted two churches and have 35+ years of ministry experience. She understands the vital role that women play in starting a church and founded Stadia's ministry called Bloom (stadia.cc\bloom). Bloom's mission is to empower women to maximize their role in starting churches. Debbie and the Bloom team connect, empower and lead hundreds of women across the United States. Debbie loves to play tennis, pickle ball and most of all spend time with family, including: their daughter, Melanie, her husband Jade and daughters, Cora and Celia, and their son, Tom, and his wife Stephanie, and their daughter, Emilia.

## LAUGHING WITH GOD

The year was 1986. My hair was big, our bank account was small and the Sunday had arrived where we would be asking our incredible church family to sacrifice even more than they already were. The goal set for the day was $5,000. The often-referenced wealth of the '80s was glaringly absent in our reality.

My husband Tom and I had planted Southbrook Christian Church 20 months before this day. Prior to and during those 20 months, God had been busy doing amazing things in our community. There was no doubt this was what we were made for, but in the midst of all of the goodness, the pressing need for more financial resources, was evident. We needed our infant church to take that next step toward maturity—it was time for our first church-wide giving campaign.

In preparation for this significant milestone, Tom and I prayed, planned, talked and brainstormed about what our personal financial commitment would be. We arrived at the amount of $1,000. Yes, in spite of having one baby and one 2-year-old who both depended on us for everything, we believed God was telling us that our third child—this church plant—deserved one thousand currently non-existent dollars from us. If we were going to ask our people to take a leap of faith, then we were going to jump off the cliff just ahead of them. But we couldn't help but ask, "How on earth would we find this kind of money?"

We begged God, "Show us You are in this! Give us some way to know this is from You." We also began to plan out how God might lead us to this $1,000 goal. Possible action steps included:

- Tom wanted to sell his plasma. I immediately rejected this idea—I didn't even need to pray. This church has our sweat and tears, but our literal blood is staying in our bodies, thank you very much!
- We could have a Garage Sale.
- We could try to find something of greater value (beyond our Garage Sale items) to sell.

Tom's brain started humming. In our garage there was an old train set that Tom's dad had purchased for him when he was three years old. Years later after his Dad's passing, his Mom had delivered the train to our garage and there it had remained. The train was pulled out, shined up and readied for an exhibit. To his surprise, the very first collector's shop Tom entered immediately offered him $500. Thank goodness this was not Tom's first rodeo. He politely thanked the gentleman for his offer and headed back home. If a walk off the street instantly garnered a $500 offer, then this little train must be worth something.

Days later Tom was with Scott, a friend from church, and mentioned the train adventure. Scott proceeded to share that he had a friend who was going to a Model Train Fair in York, Pennsylvania the next day and shared his contact information. Without delay Tom drove to the friend's house, handed over the train and explained what we were planning to do with any money received from its sale. We questioned our sanity for trusting a stranger with our prize but we quickly reminded ourselves Who was in control. The following day the call came and Tom's train had sold for $1,200. More than the $1,000 we had already committed, we were given an extra $200 for good measure!

What began on that faith-filled Sunday resulted in a $5,001 total offering from our church. Yes, you caught that, right? The church gave exactly $1 over our needed amount. This experience continued to shape the life and ministry of our young church. Following that campaign our monthly offering more than doubled which allowed our baby church to finally become self-supporting at 20 months old. Self-sustainability, as all church planters know, is such a monumental step in your church's story. "The Guts and Glory of Reversals" were lavishly illustrated in our lives as we watched a childhood toy pay the grown-up sized cost, created by a pledge made in good faith.

Together we learned to trust God even when the challenge seems beyond the realm of reality. Esther also faced an incredible challenge that must have seemed beyond the realm of her reality—especially as a young, Jewish orphan girl. Just as we used what we had in our garage, Esther surrendered what tools she had to make an impact. Just as we felt a bit foolish for believing that a toy train could make a difference, I imagine Esther felt foolish for believing God could use her to rescue her Hebrew family. 1 Corinthians 1:27 reminds us, "but God has chosen the foolish things of the world to shame the wise, and God has chosen the weak things of the world to shame the things which are strong." We, like Esther, were weak and perhaps foolish but God made us strong and wise as we placed ourselves in His hands.

As anyone who has a decent amount of church planting years under their belt knows, the deliriously "happy endings" one experiences are rarely the true endings. So, fast forward 10 years with me to the late spring of 1996, at our 2nd church plant in Princeton, New Jersey. This church plant we were leading had been meeting at a local high school. There were many positives about this set-up: no "churchy feel," high visibility and conducive rooms to transform into children's ministry spaces. In the nineties, however, the open space concept in schools was booming, making it costly to rent and even more expensive to air condition the building. So we never did. Yes, you read that right. In our 3½ years we had never been able to afford air conditioning.

The dual use space meant extensive setup and teardown every week. The precious people of our church were loading and unloading and then attending a service drenched in sweat while the rest of the church had only a slightly cooler experience due to the lack of manual labor. Then we'd all show up the next weekend to do it over again and again and again. Beyond the sweaty set up, situations at the school began to also impact our Sunday gatherings. At our high school every year there was a notorious "Senior Prank" tradition. The Senior Class of 1996 decided to step it up a notch by releasing rats in the halls of their beloved Alma Mater. Yes, the scenario unfolds exactly as you just imagined. Tom was preaching on stage one Sunday when the rats ran across the front row under the lifted legs of the people sitting in shock and then fled out the side door. The staff chased them down the hallway trying to keep this crazy Sunday as normal as possible. Bottom line—between the heat and the rats—it was time to move!

At the time we had $1,000 in our land and building fund. In our minds, however, we lived in an Ivy League town so a building campaign with this church plant should be a piece of cake. In spite of that reality, our team was becoming discouraged. We were all praying God would reveal what our next step should be. Then the call came—a church in the area had decided to close its doors. They felt called to give their property to another area church as a part of the legacy of the faithful members who had worshiped there for so many years. Somehow, our church plant was placed on their short list, along with two other churches.

To be perfectly honest, I was incredibly skeptical. I feared that the building would be so "churchy" that it would threaten the DNA God had built into our church, which was to be a safe place for seekers with church baggage. I felt intensely protective of our little church, so Tom and I decided to go check out the building. We rounded the turn to find the property completely blocked by trees. "Easy fix," Tom quipped. As we passed through the wooded area, the property opened up to a beautiful facility that was exactly what we were wanting. It was perfect. As we walked into the building, I knew deep in my heart that it was exactly where we were supposed to be. It was such a holy moment.

As we walked through the halls, the enormity of it all began to settle. It was not just the perfect building; it was completely furnished, including fully equipped children's classrooms and, as a cherry on top, a baby grand piano on the stage (which in that decade was a rare bonus for any church plant). We were meant for this location, but we were also one of three churches being considered. My heart was heavy as I began to pray diligently for this property.

Consumed with the hope that this could be God's beautiful provision for this vital crossroads in our church's story I would drive to the property late at night and pour my heart out to God. I truly believed this was where we were supposed to be. Then finally the phone rang. As unexpectedly as the initial call had come, it was with the same stealth that the deed was done. Our little church was chosen and we were left speechless by how God had moved.

Through all of this we also learned, like the book of Esther, "It's Okay to Laugh." How can one not laugh at rats grabbing stage time, sweat stained servants and the ludicrous optimism of a $1,000 building fund in the shadows of an Ivy League university? Through the laughter we also learned the importance of prayer. Just as Esther asked Mordecai and the people of Israel to pray and fast for her as she prepared to face the King, we prayed fervently for this church building. I will never forget those moments sitting in my car on that property and begging God to give this space to our church. We learned, like Esther, that God can be trusted with the precious dreams formed deep within our souls.

That audacious $5,001 offering back in 1986 propelled Southbrook Christian Church into healthy growth, which has continued to this day where over 5,000 people gather to learn, serve, and love the One who loved them first. That devoted group of believers who kept showing up week in and week out in Princeton in 1996 are still there—gathering, praying and sitting on a multi-million dollar piece of property, on a major highway, for which we never paid a penny. We used what we had, prayed for what we didn't and learned to laugh with God through it all. And I believe God's laugh is always the loudest.

## CHI CHI OKWU

Chi Chi Okwu is a Senior Church Advisor for World Vision USA (worldvision.org), working with church leaders, churches and parachurch organizations to build strategic partnerships and increase social justice engagement globally. She is passionate about issues relating to faith and justice, specifically in the areas of race, gender and reconciliation. Chi Chi is a graduate of the University of Alabama and has a Masters Degree in Public Health and Business Administration. She has also completed graduate work at North Park Seminary focusing on Urban Ministry. Previously she worked in healthcare consulting and most recently as Associate Pastor at Willow Creek Chicago, serving as a part of the teaching team and overseeing all social justice, community group, communications and care ministries. She enjoys speaking and writing on topics relating to faith and justice. Chi Chi resides in Chicago and enjoys traveling, cooking, watching sports and spending quality time with friends and family.

## WHERE MY PAIN MEETS GOD'S LOVE

I was laying in bed on a Saturday desperately trying to hide from the world. The last several days we had seen, via video, two African-American men shot by police. A peaceful protest had turned violent when a single shooter decided to take matters into his own hands and kill five police officers. The dialogue surrounding these events was incredibly divisive and painful. I was wrecked. I couldn't stop the tears from coming. I was angry, devastated and afraid to look at the news for fear of what I would read next. I did not know how to process the pain I was feeling. A sense of dread started to creep over me as I realized I could not stay in bed forever. Sunday was coming. I was going to have to find a way to lead a diverse congregation through this time of turmoil…again. I felt like I had nothing left to give. The text from my boss, and dear friend, finally came, "How should we address this on Sunday?" I put my phone down. I couldn't respond yet. I had no words. I couldn't even leave my bed much less plan a service. I was angry, I was terrified and I was in pain. Pictures of my brother, nephew and black male friends crowded my mind. Could they be next? I did not want to speak of hope and reconciliation. I knew, however, that I didn't have that luxury. I said a hasty prayer to my Creator, "This one is on you, God."

After a phone call and a flurry of emails, I found myself staring at the dreaded blank screen of my computer. Our team had decided I would write a reflection for the Sunday service addressing the events of the previous week. There was just one problem. I wasn't feeling hopeful. I wasn't ready to fight for justice or be pastoral. I was feeling too much pain; I was too raw. I couldn't trust myself to speak a message of unity and hope to a diverse congregation. But as I stared at the screen I sensed God saying, "Write from your pain and write from my love." I started writing and the tears began to flow. I wrote about the truth of my pain and my deep, yet uncertain hope for a future that reflected the kingdom of God.

I don't usually get nervous about public speaking. Being a pastor you get used to it very quickly; but on that Sunday I was nervous. I walked on stage, heart racing, hands trembling and palms sweating. As I started to speak through my pain and fear, God met me there. I spoke about my crippling fear, my blackness and my femininity. I called our congregation to lament the sin of white supremacy and reminded all of us that God desires oneness, love and unity. When we hurt each other we hurt ourselves. As I spoke, God reminded me that my blackness and femininity affords me a different and valuable view of the world. I was created in the image of God, reflecting the diversity of the Creator. My heritage, my gender, my pain matters to God and can be used by God to build up the kingdom of God.

The story of Esther has always been very special to me. It was one of few stories I was told as a child with a woman as the hero. Today, the story of Esther still makes me want to stand up and cheer. Esther, a woman of color, stands up to a king in resistance. She allows her connection to her people and their pain to move her. She then uses her position to speak truth to power.

In Esther 4:4 we see Esther in great distress because of the pain of Mordecai. As she grows to understand the pain and oppression of her people she is moved to action. Rather than limiting her, Esther's story, pain and connection to her people actually make her the right person for the job. Her response to Mordecai's challenge is unforgettable. Esther boldly resolves, "I will go to the king, even though it is against the law. And if I perish, I perish" (Esther 4:16). She risks everything to speak on behalf of her people, to speak truth to power.

I don't pretend to know what it's like to risk my life to speak out like Esther, but her story is inspirational to me and I go back to it often. As a woman in ministry I can often forget that God's calling on me does not exclude the pain and struggle I experience. My voice is born from my connection to humanity, the limits that society tries to place on me and the struggle to resist and exist in the world.

There is an innate desire in all of us to live into the calling God has given us. For many women and people of color that means going against cultural expectations. Our voice may be hard for some to hear because it is often a prophetic reminder of the way of the kingdom. But it is the voice God has given us—a voice that speaks to the now and the not yet; a voice that will ring throughout the generations; a voice that comes from the shaken, the broken, the fearful and the fearless; a voice that speaks of pain and the love of God; a voice that proclaims, "Thy kingdom come!" Esther is a reminder that regardless of what society tries to dictate, when God places us in places of leadership it is not a mistake or accident. We must speak up and speak truth. It's a reminder that our pain and our story is often the very thing that will push us to work towards seeing God's kingdom here on earth. God wants to use our voice to tear down the systems that go against God's will. It's a reminder that when we surrender to the Creator our voice can become a catalyst for hope, healing and freedom.

> *And who knows but that you have come to your royal position for such a time as this?"*
>
> — Esther 4:14

ANONYMOUS

CHAPTER THREE

# MORDECAI
## A GOOD MENTOR IS HARD TO FIND

"What are you waiting for? You start it." I will never forget those words from my Youth Pastor when I was a sophomore in high school. Our Wednesday night youth service was supposed to start in two minutes and our Youth Pastor was nowhere to be found. I, however, knew exactly where he was. It was my job to know. I served as the "Program Team Leader" of our weekly worship services, meaning I was in charge of making sure the service started on time, transitions were smooth and everything was in place. The first person scheduled to start the service on this particular night was our Youth Pastor. But he was in a meeting with several adult leaders in our church. Slightly agitated and anxious, I wondered to myself, "Why does he always schedule this meeting right up until the time we are supposed to start?" Knock, knock, knock. I hesitatingly interrupted the meeting to remind him of the time. "What are you waiting for, Dori? You start it." And just like that I heard one of my Mordecais say, "For such a time as this."

Mordecai is an interesting person in the book of Esther. His name derives from the Babylonian god Marduk, yet he is undoubtedly Jewish, of the tribe of Benjamin.[1] The name fits, however, as he also lives between two worlds. Like Esther, he is learning to navigate between the sackcloth of Jewish mourning and the robe of the Persian palace. While he appears to occupy some seat of significance in the citadel of Susa (2:5, 3:3), unlike Esther he

---

1  B. W. Anderson, B.M. Metzger & R.E. Murphy, *The New Oxford Annotated Bible with the Apocryphal/Deuterocanonical Books* (New York: Oxford University Press, 1991). Note on Esther 2:5 and 7:11.

is of no real significance to King Ahasuerus—even after he saves the King's life (2:21-3:1). He is conflicted at times regarding the best way to live in this 'in between' space. On the one hand, he encourages Esther not to reveal her Jewish nationality to the King (2:10). On the other, he does not hesitate to reveal his own Jewishness to the King's servants (3:4).[2] Mordecai also shares a similarity with Vashti as he refuses to follow the King's command to bow down to Haman (3:2). Yet unlike Vashti, he loudly weeps when he learns of the national consequences of his refusal (4:1).[3] In some ways his actions seem well calculated and in other ways he appears to make quick decisions without thinking of the consequences. He is passionate, loyal, inspirational and intelligent. While at other times he is rash, arrogant, fearful and foolish. Bottom line—Mordecai is human. All mentors are.

> *And the things you have heard me say in the presence of many witnesses entrust to reliable people who will also be qualified to teach others.*
>
> — 2 Timothy 2:2

There are countless books, conferences, seminars and sermons about what it means to be a mentor and how to identify the "reliable people" who need to be mentored. One could argue that Esther's maturation from the adopted girl who followed the advice of her cousin, to the Queen who later gave him advice, reveals how Mordecai was a top-notch mentor. After all, the student has become the teacher. What if, however, mentoring isn't a linear process that moves toward this one final stage? Trust me, I like linear progressions; it would make mentoring and being mentored so much easier. But have you ever wondered why you can follow the same steps and get different results when it comes to mentoring? People are fluid and the end results of mentoring are not as easily measureable as we would like them to be. So rather than a linear framework, what if mentoring actually comes in waves? With ebbs and flows, the tide comes in and goes back out. We think the person we are mentoring is ready, but then the mentee needs more time. We think we are ready, but then we need more time. The same man who gives the legendary "For such a time is this" speech was just minutes before weeping in sackcloth in fear of the future for his people. I think we

---

2  Betchel, *Esther*, 46.

3  Day, *Esther*, 83

have just as much to learn from Mordecai's foolishness as his inspirational leadership. Mordecai is human. All mentors are.

As mentioned in the verse above, the one qualification Timothy suggests we look for in a mentor is reliability. In Greek, the word we read as "reliable" can also mean "faithful" or "trustworthy." So often I hear how difficult it is to find a good mentor. What if a good mentor is hard to find because we aren't really looking for faithful, reliable, trustworthy people. Of course, that's what we say we want. But what if we are actually looking for perfect people without any faults? That is definitely hard to find. Better said, a perfect mentor is impossible to find.

While I love telling the story of how my Youth Pastor challenged me to step on the stage and start our youth service that night, I also have stories of how I broke down emotionally under the weight of my perfectionist tendencies and the expectations placed upon me at such a young age. Did I mention I was only 15-years-old and the youth group was 150+ students? Just as I have stories of the impact this Youth Pastor made in the lives of the students in our church, I also have stories of seeing him make mistakes in other areas of his life. I don't fault him for this. I just realize what isn't mentioned enough in church—he was human. He made mistakes and at times he failed me. At the same time, he was faithful, he was trustworthy and he helped lead me to the day when God called me into ministry. He was reliable, but he was not perfect.

I hope I will always have room for mentors in my life. I desperately need the words and wisdom of people who have gone before me, especially the women who have been planting churches and leading ministries long before I knew their names. As I grow older I have also grown into the role of being a mentor. At times it has been a messy process. Moving from being the intern to having interns is quite a shift. I have had to repeat the phrase that one of my mentors, Sue Lueders, once told me—"You don't know what they don't know." Finding reliable young women and men to mentor has been a challenge. But I must confess, it has mostly been a challenge because I often keep looking for perfection. I have expected what I myself cannot be. Mordecai reminds me to give grace both to my mentors and to the people I have mentored. Other than Jesus, I will not find perfection. If I look close enough, however, I will find the faithful, the trustworthy and the reliable.

In the following stories you will learn more about the Mordecais who have come alongside of church planting women as well as the Mordecais who are church planting women. Some of the mentors and mentees are women, some men, some intentional and some unexpected. But they are all significant, reliable, faithful and undoubtedly human.

**KARRIE THOMAS**

Karrie Thomas is a pastor, missionary, singer, photographer, writer and daughter of Christ. She is passionate about sharing God's story and finds that all of her roles allow her to do just that. After nearly 10 years of working with student ministries in Indianapolis, Phoenix and Boulder, in 2011 Karrie and her husband Aaron planted Restore Church (wearerestore.com), a missional Stadia church plant in the city of Silver Spring, Maryland. Along with their three boys, they love living just a few miles north of the White House where ministry life in a big city is always an adventure.

## HUMBLE BOLDNESS

> *Mordecai had a cousin named Hadassah, whom he had brought up because she had neither father nor mother. This young woman, who was also known as Esther, had a lovely figure and was beautiful. Mordecai had taken her as his own daughter when her father and mother died....Every day he walked back and forth near the courtyard of the harem to find out how Esther was and what was happening to her.*
>
> — Esther 2:7, 11

Mordecai seemed, for all intents and purposes, Esther's father. He didn't biologically parent her and she never referred to him as "Father," but he raised, loved and mentored her as his own. He guided and watched over her as a father would. Did he know this would be his life? Did he know he was essentially preparing a beautiful little girl to become a queen who would change the course of history for the entire Jewish race? Probably not, but still he confidently yet humbly poured into her.

Just as Mordecai found himself in an unexpected position of influence, I often find myself in leadership situations that seemingly "fall into my lap." I never imagined I'd mentor or teach anyone. Growing up I wanted to be a TV anchorwoman. I'm embarrassed to admit it now, but I even had my television-appropriate name picked out: Karrie Day. I dreamed of a perfectly coiffed hairstyle, writing and reading bits of news from a teleprompter, and smiling and frowning at just the right moments. I certainly wanted to deliver news with passion and truth leading the way, but didn't imagine myself leading others beyond the camera. Instead, here I am embracing life as a mother of three boys and co-pastor of a D.C.-area church with my husband, Aaron. God works in mysterious ways and continues to surprise me.

In the summer of 2013, Aaron and I were juggling parenting and pastoring duties with our newly planted church in downtown Silver Spring, Maryland. We took turns swapping time at home caring for our little boys, and taking on church work and meetings at local coffee shops. One morning just after Aaron left the house for the day, I was awakened by sounds of an angry 6-year-old pounding his fists against the wall and wailing as loud as he could.

I was a new parent, and these sounds were alarming to say the least. I anxiously ran down the stairs to check on my son only to find him excitedly punching a toddler mattress we'd temporarily leaned against the wall the night before. I grabbed his little arms asking, "Ty?! Are you okay, honey?" A toothy grin began forming on his sweet little freckled face as he responded with a simple, "Yeah!" and went back to hitting the mattress.

It may sound crazy, but as a parent I'd expected to understand every emotion and desire my kids would have. This time, however, I didn't. My son was thoroughly enjoying this "match" between him and the mattress, but my favorite childhood pastimes—dancing in circles and rocking babydolls—weren't helpful to understand his behavior. This seemingly small moment was significant for me as a mother and as a leader. A whisper in my heart calmed my nerves saying, "He is a unique person. You are raising someone who is wired differently than you."

Relying only on my experiences and feelings, I would have done my best to calm my son and then instruct him to use his hands for more productive and loving things than punching. I decided, instead, to keep the mattress there for a few days for his enjoyment. For those three days he was easily Mom's #1 Fan. And over those three days I realized the honor and gift I'd been given to play a small but significant role in helping to raise him, giving him the space to be who God made him to be.

When my boys need honest feedback, encouragement or correction, they know to expect it from me. In parenting, the relationship and expectations are clear. But so many of us are called to lead others that don't really "have" to follow us. They don't have to sit in time out or write "I will obey my mother" when they choose not to follow our advice. Yet, we're called to lead them, providing feedback, encouragement and correction. To do so, we must rely on different methods.

My first official foray into vocational ministry included a position in which I was responsible for leading several people, both men and women. This experience brought some painful lessons. Barely into my 20s, I didn't know how to humbly but confidently lead anyone, but especially men. I had tried to take a strong lead in a few situations but was met with harsh resistance—and it stung. These were more than "emotional speed bumps." Even though there were plenty of fruitful moments, the few uncomfortable incidences in those first years, unfortunately, led to my cowardly leadership of others for a while. Many years passed before I noticed fruitfulness in my leadership because I'd failed to embrace God's leadership lessons for me in that experience.

Thankfully, God used these experiences to teach me that mentoring doesn't have to be hierarchical, and perhaps it shouldn't be. It may sound simple, but this idea completely transformed how I communicate the burdens and truths God has shown me to the people I mentor. Mentorship is equal parts humble submission to God's voice, and strong, tactful delivery of wisdom. I love how Mordecai and Esther seem to have an equal exchange of respect and honor for one another's voice, just as mature believers should. In Esther 2:20 it says, "For she continued to follow Mordecai's instructions as she had done when he was bringing her up." A few chapters later we learn how Mordecai equally submitted to her role as his queen when she'd tasked him with fasting for a few days. "So Mordecai went away and carried out all of Esther's instructions" (Esther 4:17). In a culture where hierarchy among genders was assumed, we see Mordecai and Esther respecting each other and learning from each other.

In full evidence of God's lavish grace, I've continued to be entrusted with leadership roles since the fumbling attempts of my 20s. For the past two years, specifically, I've had the honor of helping prepare my friends Andy and Janet, a husband and wife team, to plant a church. In many instances, I've been inspired to share godly truth with Andy. Though he's had just as many years of ministry experience, his humble, teachable spirit has allowed him to learn church planting lessons from me. Through this, both Andy and my husband have encouraged me not only to teach and guide, but also to do it loudly with confidence. What a gift!

There is tremendous value in embracing humility and submission to God's leading as we step boldly into the leading roles we are given. Today I heard a song that has stuck with me, reminding me of the freedom found when we lead through Christ. "Jesus, Jesus, how I trust Him! How I've proved Him O'er and O'er. Jesus, Jesus, precious Jesus! Oh, for grace to trust Him more!"

**SUZI LANTZ**

Suzi Lantz is a book-loving resource who always has a good read to recommend! Suzi is the Missional Community Director at RiverTree Christian Church's Jackson Campus (rivertreejackson.com) in Massillon, Ohio. She loves helping connect people to discipleship relationships and to living on mission with God. She is married to Jason Lantz, pastor of RiverTree Christian Church, and mother to Caris and Joshua.

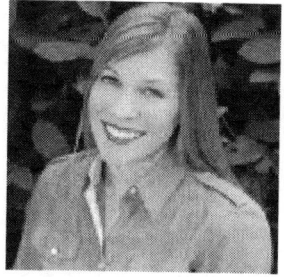

## THEY ARE THE SOLUTION, NOT YOU

"Can we schedule a time to meet up? Joe and I have been troubled over something at church that we want to talk to you about."

I instantly began to think through all the things that this young family might be finding wrong with our 1½-year-old church plant. It's funny how often our minds can create such instant critiques at the slightest mention of trouble brewing. We were vulnerable—still renting space, setting up and tearing down every week. We weren't financially sustainable and we had very few spiritual parents among the ranks. Troubling things weren't music to our ears.

"Of course, why don't you come over next week and we can discuss it."

Next week came and there they were, sitting on our back porch, lemonade in hand, looking just as nervous as we felt. Mandy and Joe were newer to the church but had jumped in with both feet and had instantly become a part of the family. They were passionate about the mission, excited about new opportunities and fiercely devoted to their family of five. The small talk had come to an awkward pause, so I directed the conversation back to "the trouble mentioned on the phone" which at this point in my mind had become akin to the sinking of the Titanic.

Mandy glanced at Joe and then launched in, "We love our missional community and everything that is currently happening at LoveCanton, but we are having a hard time with the lack of direct investment in our kids at SW Village."[4] They had chosen to connect with a missional community full of ambitious college students and young married adults. Currently this Village had no set plan for kids.

We couldn't argue with the problems they were experiencing. Mandy mentioned loading up a van full of toys for every gathering and something about a room the size of a closet where one of them would be banished with the kids when they got too wild. Yikes! We would definitely plan on talking to their Village leader about that arrangement. I was feeling defeated and guilty. The kind of guilt that, on the one hand, you know isn't yours to bear, but on the other, if only it were possible to do more, be more, or be enough?

It was at that moment when the Holy Spirit spoke powerfully to my heart and mind, "They are the solution, not you."

My husband Jason was in the middle of apologizing for their experience and explaining the development of missional communities and how this is something we needed to figure out when I broke in, "You two are the first people who have mentioned this gap in the church, and I'm wondering if it is because God has brought you here to be a part of the solution. We have been so busy serving the undervalued in our community and being on mission with all of the young college students, singles and young couples who are just crazy enough to live on mission that we haven't thought enough about how to disciple families."

Their immediate response was akin to, "Um, no thank you. We came to you because we want you to fix this problem. Do something for our kids or we will most likely have to find something else." The conversation ended that night, politely but with a strong feeling that we better figure out something for kids in missional communities or we'd be absent one family.

In the next few weeks we asked local college students to help with the kids during their gatherings and stocked them with boxes of supplies, toys and

---

4 LoveCanton is a church plant launched by RiverTree Church in partnership with Stadia. "Villages" or "Missional Communities" are small churches that live life together. They meet every other Sunday at different locations around Canton with anywhere from 20-40 people attending.

lots of coloring books. But I still couldn't shake the message the Holy Spirit had spoken to me that night, "They are the solution, not you."

God is gracious; in the next six months we were having another conversation on our back porch, where Mandy and Joe informed us that God spoke to them and they wanted to start a missional community focused on discipling whole families to be on mission with God.

There are many voices who had begun to speak in Mandy's life at that time. I recognize that I am only one of those voices. But the joy of watching, from an insider view, what God would do in her heart and through her hands in the next few years inspires gratitude in me.

In 1 Timothy 4:6, Paul reminds us when God calls out a gift in a person, and you are the one to give words to it, then it becomes your responsibility to fan the flame. This fanning began through our bi-weekly huddle where our missional community leaders would find themselves in our living room, coffee in hand, answering the questions –"What is God saying to you and what are you going to do about it?"

Those precious times of being led in the Word and guided by the Spirit cultivated the heart of a leader in Mandy and refined the shepherding gifts that Joe possessed. She had been a stay-at-home mom for years and had found great joy in caring for her young children, being the best homemade bread-maker I've ever known. God, however, was calling Mandy into deeper waters of understanding Him, of being used by Him, of discipling others for Him and speaking for Him. She needed a friend and someone who understood the complexity of balance, patience and being a woman in ministry. And I was blessed to be that friend.

Reflecting back on the two years of Mandy's initial step into leadership and the time I have invested in her, there are a few things I learned about mentoring relationships:

First, have time and make time. Mentoring takes both intentionally planned time and random access. There were times when we had regularly scheduled huddles, training times and one-on-one coaching meetings that were intentional. But, much of the information and experiential wisdom I passed on to Mandy came through random texts, emails, and calls that flooded in when she found herself in a new situation that she hadn't experienced before. It was in those times that my primary focus was listening. Being a sounding board and not a megaphone of advice was the posture I took. She knew what to do and God was teaching her, but she needed a vote of confidence and reassurance from time to time, as we all do.

Second, don't try to make them you. I realized early on that Mandy and I, though both women in missional ministry, are wired very differently. On our best days, she's a quarterback and I'm a coach. Truthfully, I had to fight the desire to try to make her like me. I'm research driven, cautious and run a tight agenda. She's bold, innovative and flows with the Spirit more naturally.

At times, I'd see her shine and I would mist up with tears thinking about how far she had come. To be honest, however, there were also twinges of jealousy at who she was and the capacity she possessed. She is like the energizer bunny who keeps going and going and going! It was vital to acknowledge our differences and ask God for direction over what things I was to pass along to her and what things required others to fill in the gap.

Last, connect them with other people in your network. It takes a village to build a leader. God will call you to mentor someone and invest intentionally, but you are not the end all be all. Connect that person to others in your network so they can be developed more fully. We are the body of Christ, and each one of us plays a role. Getting to connect Mandy and Joe to some of the people who have helped cultivate Jason and me has been such a joy.

It's been more than seven years since that conversation on our back porch and in that time I've been able to see how right the Holy Spirit was when He whispered to me, "They are the solution, not you." Mandy and Joe started a family-centered missional community, and it had an impact on nearly every family that entered our church in the next few years. They developed leaders so that it multiplied into three more family-centered missional communities. She was my apprentice as Developer and Equipper over all of the Missional Communities at LoveCanton and eventually was hired to replace me when I moved into another role. She has become an incredible teacher, gifting many congregations with her humorous and passionate sermons.

Now, because God knew what He was doing when He whispered, "They are the answer, not you," Mandy is the lead pastor at LoveCanton, the church we started through our blood, sweat, and tears. God allowed us to see His hand in her life and fan the gifts He had given her into a flame. Jason and I were called to lead the network church that LoveCanton is now part of and Mandy is carrying the vision God gave us into a new place. She is working to ensure families are reached and kids have the opportunity to know Jesus and be used by him.

I stand amazed at how a simple conversation initiated through a complaint brought about a woman who is changing the world around her for Jesus.

## LAURA BUFFINGTON

Laura Buffington cares deeply about the words and pictures we use to tell the story of God at work in the world. Laura is the teaching pastor at Southbrook Christian Church (southbrook.org) in Dayton, Ohio. She also is the content developer for Rebel Pilgrim Creative Agency (rebelpilgrim. com) in Cincinnati, Ohio. She enjoys partnering with a non-profit group, Bespoken Live (bespokenlive.org), who hosts crafted storytelling events to help people see the value in telling and listening to good stories. She loves running to good music and telling stories around all kinds of tables.

## RUNNING TOWARD WISDOM

Many of my earliest memories come from life inside the church—both the building and the people. In most of these memories I am resistant. My resistance started at home as my mother battled to get me into a dress with frilly socks and uncomfortable shoes. Upon arrival I remember fighting with the boys and folding my arms across my chest when I was supposed to be making hand motions to songs. I remember trying to climb the poles that held together the wooden curtains separating the third graders from the fourth. I did whatever I could to keep my time in church interesting until the moment of my inevitable escape—sneaking out the back door. During one such grand escape, convinced no one would see me leave, I remember someone waving at me.

But instead of feeling caught, I felt seen. Tricia waved at me and smiled, letting me know she saw me breaking away and she might have even understood. She was the youth pastor's wife, though she might resist any association we have with that role or title. Honestly, there might have been a few days she wanted to sneak out too.

I kept coming back to church, scowling, skulking. Tricia kept coming too, starting conversations with me so that eventually we were hanging out all the time. We went to the mall, to the park, to their family's house for dinner or games.

By the time I was deep into the identity politics and emotional turmoil of middle school life, her friendship became a shelter for me. To her credit I had no idea she was developing this friendship for any grand purpose. I did not know I was being mentored. I thought I had just stumbled into some fortunate space in the world that was filled with guidance, encouragement and wisdom.

Over the years she listened when I told hard stories. She spoke good truth to me when I believed false stories. She let me into her life enough to see what a mature faith looked like, even on days when it wasn't easy.

When I was a junior in high school Tricia and her husband Greg suffered a great loss. We sat together the Sunday after and she opened up the pages of her Bible to show me a tear-stained page. She told me the story of reading Scripture through tears, showing me that grief and faith could live in the same space. Years later when I faced my own grief, I remembered those pages and I let the faith-filled, hope-filled, sorrow-filled tears fall.

When it came time for me to make decisions about college and career with all of the mystery of the future, she asked me good questions and confirmed the moves I made toward ministry and meaning. There was a moment along the way when Tricia let me know that being mentored was not the end game of our friendship. She made it clear to me that I needed to look around and give away whatever I had received. That's when the jig was up.

I figured out that this had all been on purpose. Every conversation, every confession, every peaceful moment of good company, was a part of the way God designs the kingdom—anything we have is meant to be given away. The rhythm was laid out: look ahead, behind and beside for people who need to be seen and heard.

Aside from the very specific support Tricia and Greg gave me over the years, I realize now what a gift it was to receive mentoring at such a young age. The kind of space they made for me became the space I sought and still seek. It's that rarefied space where we set aside pride and practice confession and guidance. It's not easy to allow others to edit or correct our lives. They helped me build the emotional muscle memory to accept the "trusted wounds" that Proverbs prescribe for the faithful (Proverbs 26:7).

Proverbs also tells us that wise people are supposed to love this correction. Even more than loving it, they're meant to search it out. They're supposed to look for people to correct them actively. Rather than running from, fighting against or hiding away from correction, they are expected to listen, absorb and embrace it. If we don't practice this with each other, if we don't listen to each other and correct each other, it will get harder for us to hear and receive the kind of correction that comes from God.

If we have said that we want our lives to look like the life of Jesus, that's going to mean opening ourselves up to change. It's going to mean we hold our lives up next to the description of how life could be in Scripture and we make sure we start looking more and more like that. It's going to mean when we read the Bible, we're open to hearing where we have failed and where we might be lost. It means if we're passionless or focusing our lives on things that don't matter, then we let the Spirit of God speak to us and wake us up.

Mordecai sees what Esther cannot. I have known for a very long time that I may need someone else to shine the light a little further down the road than I can see. I have moved through the world knowing I might need some collective wisdom to know exactly what time it is and how I can live up to the moment. Practicing this with mentors, beginning with Tricia and Greg, taught me how to receive this from the Spirit of God all along the way.

**LIZ GENTRY**

Liz Gentry is a compassionate pastor and dynamic preacher who loves helping everyone feel welcomed and valued in the church. During her time at Milligan College (milligan.edu), Liz interned with numerous student ministries across the country, including Mountain Christian Church in Joppa, Maryland (mountaincc.org), Plainfield Christian Church in Plainfield, Indiana (plainfieldchristian.com) and North Ridge Community Church in Johnson City, Tennessee (northridgenetwork. com). Currently, Liz is the Pastor of Hospitality at NewStory Church (newstorychicago.com), a Stadia partner church in Chicago, Illinois. She is also working on her Masters in Theology and Mission at Northern Seminary (seminary.edu). She is a budding painter, finds great joy in bird-watching and continues to dream about planting a church one day wherever God may lead.

## CLEARING AWAY THE COBWEBS

During my junior year at Milligan College I decided to spend a semester at Mountain Christian Church in Joppa, Maryland. I had applied and been accepted to be a part of their internship program for college students seriously considering vocational ministry. By the time I arrived at Mountain I was sure of my calling and excited to gain insight and tools for ministry.

Specific to my calling, I was 100% convinced God had led me to youth ministry. I had a passion for seeing teenagers draw closer to Christ and loved being a part of helping them get there. But as often happens, God had another idea in mind. The Lord would give me a dream I never expected possible.

As the semester began, I sat down with Ethan Magness, the program director at the time, to develop the syllabus for my internship experiences, activities, and responsibilities. I had lots of ideas—writing curriculum, leading a small group and anything and everything related to youth ministry. Without my input Ethan added, "preaching" to my syllabus. Before the semester ended I would preach twice for our middle school and high school services.

While I didn't necessarily have stage fright, preaching was definitely out of my comfort zone. Therefore, when the time came for my first sermon I was a nervous wreck. I wrote multiple drafts and even preached it out loud to Ethan and the Middle School Pastor for their feedback. Needless to say, preaching to Ethan was even more nerve-racking than preaching to a room full of middle school students. I knew his critique would be much more intense. Mountain had a top notch preaching team, and Ethan Magness was no exception. He held high standards for interns and I held his opinion in high regard.

Then came a conversation I will always remember. I had just preached my second sermon for our students and I had a meeting with Ethan to debrief the sermon. He began giving feedback as he always would, some good things and a lot to improve. Then suddenly Ethan stopped talking, looked at me, and said something I'll never forget, "Ok, now I don't say this to interns very often, but in your case I need to. You're a really good preacher. You could be a great preacher. You just have to do it more often."

I was floored. Ethan Magness, a phenomenal preacher and beloved mentor, just told me I could be a great preacher one day! I wasn't sure what to do with the information at the time. In fact, while I was incredibly honored by his compliment, I scoffed, "Yeah, alright Ethan, but who would let me preach on a regular basis? Not my church back home or in Tennessee!" To which he replied, "Who cares who lets you preach?! Preach to the birds if you have to! But preach, and preach often, because you're gifted to do so."

I don't remember a whole lot about the feedback he gave me on that particular sermon. What I do remember is leaving his office that day with tears welling up in my eyes. Could I really be a preacher? It was a dream I never expected to be possible. I grew up in a fairly typical Christian Church where women didn't lead the communion meditation, let alone preach the sermon. God blessed me, however, with a mother who also served in ministry. From early on both my mother and father encouraged and supported me as a minister too. But walking out of Ethan's office that day, I realized I had placed boundaries around my dreams for ministry.

I had limited assumptions about where God might be calling me. Youth ministry seemed possible. While I didn't have a female youth minister, I knew of some in non-denominational churches. Preaching, however, did not seem possible even though I had grown to love it that semester. Prior to this meeting with Ethan I had never allowed myself to even dream of the possibility of preaching regularly to a congregation. It was as if this dream for ministry was hidden behind a boarded up door covered in cobwebs. Then Ethan came, cleared away the cobwebs and ripped off the boards, making my way clear to a whole new possibility for where God might be calling me.

At my exit interview for the semester Ethan reminded me of my gift for preaching and said, "While you're good at youth ministry and could succeed in it, I don't actually think this is what you're truly passionate about. So pray about that." It wasn't until almost a year later that I realized my mentor was spot on. My love for preaching continued to grow and God slowly grew this dream into church planting. Being a church planter is a dream I never would have thought possible were it not for Ethan so many years ago.

Today, although I am not yet in the process of planting a church, I do preach and serve alongside an amazing staff team at NewStory Church in Chicago. Regardless of whether or not this dream is the dream God ultimately has for my life, my mentor's words that day made the dream possible. I no longer want to place boundaries around what I think God can do through me because of my gender. I pray, "God, what do you have for me?" and allow God to decide what is possible. Would I have ended up where I am had Ethan not revealed my gift for preaching that day? Perhaps. But like any great mentor, like Mordecai, Ethan cleared away some of the cobwebs blocking my "for such a time as this" calling.

ANONYMOUS

CHAPTER FOUR

# HAMAN
## OF MICE AND WOMEN

I'm not supposed to be here. But it'll be okay. That's how I felt as I stepped into a backstage room behind the sanctuary of a church that I had never entered. "I'm not supposed to be here. But it'll be okay." Those were the words I kept repeating to myself as I looked for an extension cord. My fellow classmates and I had planned a rally outside of the courthouse to speak out against the new school board superintendent's decision to deny tenure to several of our high school teachers and an assistant principal. We had planned everything with attention to detail—made posters, organized speakers, talked with the press—and here we were just moments before the rally would begin and we had overlooked one essential need. Power.

Where would we get electricity for the sound system? We knocked on the door of a nearby house and they kindly agreed to let us use their outlet, but we needed longer extension cords. That's when I saw an open door. Literally—it was the back door to a nearby church and it was wide open. I could hear the music of a band rehearsing and I knew this was our answer. I entered quietly and began looking for someone in charge. I didn't want to interrupt the band, so being familiar with most church buildings I began looking for an equipment closet. That's when I began to tell myself, "I'm not supposed to be here. But it'll be okay." And then I saw it—exactly what I was looking for—two long extension cords hanging on a hook in a storage closet. They were just what we needed. I grabbed them both and ran outside to the courthouse, whispering a prayer of gratitude for 'God's provision.'

Then I saw him coming. Out of the corner of my eye—a man was walking across the parking lot toward me. He was from the church and he was curious about the rally. But as we talked and he kept eyeing the orange cords on the ground, I could tell he was more interested in them. I asked him if we could borrow them to which he replied, "It looks like you already did." He angrily unplugged the two cords and began rolling them up, all while lecturing me about taking things that don't belong to you. Every ounce of the people-pleaser within me began to scream silently, "I'm really a good person. I actually intern at my church. I grew up in the church. I'm going to be a minister one day." But I remained silent, since I knew deep down he was right. I should have asked permission first rather than for forgiveness now. I wasn't supposed to be there. And it wasn't okay.[1]

> *The best-laid schemes o' mice an' men, Gang aft agley.*
>
> — Robert Burns in his poem "To a Mouse"

Or as we would say, "The best-laid plans of mice and men often go awry." As a high school senior I had made the best plan I could make, but in the end I had forgotten what was most important. It actually wasn't the two cords. It was my character. It was my integrity. I had forgotten an essential part of my humanity that separates me from a mouse. On that day in 1999, however, I must have looked like a mouse. I was anxious, timid, with quick, scurrying movements, attempting to go unnoticed in a place I didn't belong. On the one hand, I fully believe I am forgiven and shouldn't beat myself up for a mistake I made as a teenager many years ago. On the other hand, I don't want to miss the lesson I learned. It's the lesson of Haman. It's the choice between being a mouse or being fully human the way God intended. It's the choice often laid out in the book of Proverbs—to follow the way of the fool or to take the path of the wise.

So how does this lesson unfold for Haman? Every good story needs an antagonist, a foil who stands in contrast to the main character. Haman is such a man, though he often acts more like a mouse. Introduced as "Haman, the son of Hammedatha the Agagite" (3:1), thoughtful readers are prompted to remember the Amalekite people and their infamous King

---

1 In case you're curious, we ended up finding another outlet closer to the courthouse so we could continue our plans with just one small extension cord. The teachers and administrator, unfortunately, still lost their jobs despite the amateur efforts of a ragtag group of high school students who organized the "Save Our Faculty" rally in 1999 on the courthouse steps of Franklin, TN.

Agag (1 Samuel 15). It was this king along with his livestock that Saul did not destroy upon conquering the Amalekite army. Ironically, it was this choice that destroyed Saul's potential of remaining the King of Israel. And it is this story that lies underneath Haman's title as "the son of Hammedatha the Agagite." As old rivals, Haman is clearly cast as an antagonist to the Israelites.

Interestingly, however, Haman is also a minority; he is not Persian.[2] Similar to the Israelites in Persia, Haman is "not supposed to be there." But don't tell him that. Somehow he has managed to "be okay" by finding a position in the palace, gaining access to the King and eventually receiving the power that comes with the King's signet ring. You'd think this would be enough. But as one writer says, "Leaders can govern only as well as the ethical strength their personalities allow."[3] What does this mean for Haman?

There are three words to describe his personality—angry, impatient and egotistical. His name sounds like the Hebrew word *hemah* meaning "full of sound and fury."[4] Haman's rage at the mere sight of Mordecai (2:5,6) prompts him to irrationally persuade the King to punish all Jews, turning a personal tension into a corporal punishment. Then his impatience with his own edict pushes him to build an impaling pole so that he doesn't have to wait any longer to kill Mordecai. But, in the end, it is his ego that is his downfall. Pride definitely comes before his fall. (Proverbs 16:18). Not once did Haman think, "I'm not supposed to be here." From the beginning of the story Haman firmly believes he is exactly where he deserves to be in the palace and the King's only choice is to honor him above everyone else. In the end I imagine Haman walking to his execution pole and for the first time saying, "I'm not supposed to be here." But it is too late. And it is not okay.

Where do we find ourselves as church planting women within the story of Haman? First, I suppose it is easiest to see the stories of our own Hamans—people, organizations and structures that have stood in our way and served as our antagonists. Church planting comes with many

---

2 Betchel, *Esther*, 65.

3 Day, *Esther*, 114.

4 Betchel, *Esther*, 39

obstacles, some from within the 'palace walls' of our own congregations and some from outside the walls of the church. Female church planters face unique spiritual forces of darkness that are out to tear us down. Often these 'forces' come in tangible forms. But just as often they come from our own voices within our heads discouraging us, telling us to give up, belittling our significance and questioning our worth.

Second, if we are really honest with ourselves we'll also open our eyes to see the times when we have been Haman—when we have let our anger, impatience and ego get the best of us. It happens to all leaders. It happens to church planting women. The stories in this chapter reveal our struggle as we confront the Hamans in our world and as we confess the Haman in our mirrors. This is what separates us from the mice. This is where we lay our pride and our plans aside, confessing our need of a Savior. For if both the plans of mice and women can often go awry, then we need a God who knows the plans for us, a Power greater than our strongest strengths. We need to humble ourselves and admit, as it has been said, "Those most qualified to speak the gospel are those who truly know how unqualified they are to speak the gospel."[5] We must confess how "We're not supposed to be here." And at the same time hear God whisper, "But it'll be okay."

---

5  Tullian Tchividjian in Nadia Bolz-Weber, *Accidental Saints* (New York: Convergent Books, 2015), 30.

**SARAH BURNETT**

Sarah Burnett is an energetic passionate leader who loves to empower people to reach their potential in church planting. Sarah serves on the Bloom leadership team with Stadia and is gifted in utilizing technology to connect women in church planting. She was a contributing writer for Bloom Where You're Planted: Vol. 2. In partnership with Stadia, she and her husband Josh planted Revolution Annapolis (revolutionannapolis.com) in Annapolis, Maryland. Together they have three kids, Savannah, Grady and Madelyn.

## WHEN PEOPLE LEAVE

In the church planting world, leaders warn that you rarely finish a race with the people you start with at the beginning. I though we would be immune to that as church-planters. Surely if we were wise enough leaders, it would not happen to us. If it did happen to us, then I assumed it would be with people who were more of the "one foot in, one foot out" type of church-goers. I assumed those would be the ones who would eventually leave.

I never realized, however, that it would happen with some of our core people. The pain when someone who is "all in" leaves your church is unforgettable. Like a house of cards, it is scary when the bottom, foundational ones are pulled away. What do you do when the people you think you need to survive leave? A few years ago we had several of these families leave—back to back—and it felt like the whole thing would collapse.

My husband, Josh, and I met Rebecca after a 4th of July event the summer before the church started. We met with her, shared Jesus with her and she ended up being our very first baptism. She was the exact kind of person we were hoping to reach as we started our church. Her story was a huge confirmation to us that God was in this church plant. As time went on, however, and the church officially launched, we began to notice that she struggled to take direction from us, specifically from Josh.

There seemed to be an underlying attitude that she knew better than us. Her words to Josh could be either incredibly encouraging or so completely deflating. Eventually, we asked her to step down from leadership for a time so we could work on trusting one another. We committed to investing in each other and walked alongside each other for over a year in our small group. I remember one night when she stopped by our house and we had an amazingly honest conversation about how God had truly reconciled us. The future seemed bright; all seemed well.

More time passed and we began a Sunday series designed to teach people how to worship. Our church is filled with people who either haven't been to church before or haven't been to church in a long time. In light of this, we decided to use humor as a starting off point to talk about worship. We laughed at ourselves as we gave examples of the different hand positions people often use when they worship. This was all a spring board to teach what it really means when you raise your hands in praise to God. But Rebecca was not happy. She stormed out in the middle of the service, offended that we were making fun of worship. She was also angry that we had not addressed another issue that was politically hot in the news at that time.

At this point Josh and I talked again, but this time he was resolved to ask Rebecca to find another church. If she couldn't follow us as her pastors, then this wasn't going to work. It felt like the worst idea to me. I hate tension and this was definitely going to be tense. I knew enough about myself, however, to know that my desire for false peace rarely brings true peace. While I may long for harmony, confrontation is often vital to harmony.

Josh and I met with Rebecca again, and during that talk it became clear that she was doing everything in her power to force an apology from Josh. We were heartbroken. We both knew what needed to happen. Our greatest fear was that she would influence other amazing people to leave with her. She had many close, influential friendships with women at our church, and I was scared. While we knew that the healthiest thing for everyone was for Rebecca to leave, we knew we were risking a lot.

Over the course of that year, at least 10 families left our church. With every departure of a person came the arrival of pain. A close friend of mine left a couple of weeks after Rebecca and her husband. She told me in a Facebook message that she was leaving our church to help launch another church. Though this provided a reasonable excuse, I knew it was because of Rebecca's influence. It literally felt like a knife in my back. I cried a lot during that season and it became increasingly difficult for me to trust again or invest in others. What was the point? I could never measure up to the high expectations people place on pastors and church leaders. I am only human and this was hurting too much.

In the midst of such incredible pain, I was actually drawn closer than ever before to the heart of Jesus. Being hurt by others reminded me of how Jesus was hurt by Judas and Peter. I began asking myself, "How often do I hurt Jesus?" I cried out to the Lord praying and apologizing for the times I had broken his heart.

I also began to discover how to offer grace even when people hurt me. I started seeing people for who they really are—the good and the bad all mixed in—just as I began seeing myself. I even risked getting close to people again. In order to heal, it was imperative for me to grieve the loss of friendship as well as my own shortcomings. Grief allowed me to receive God's grace and comfort. I committed to praying for those who had hurt me, trying my best to extend grace.

You know what's great now? Although we don't have as many people at our church, we do have people who are committed to following the vision God has given us. We now know who's we are and what God requires of us. We are deeply loved by God, not for having an amazing church or a lot of people, but simply for who we are and because of who God is.

All that is required of us is to listen, obey and faithfully follow God alone. Obedience can be tough in the moment, but ultimately it provides such incredible peace. Josh recently said to me, "Would you rather obey what God is telling you to do, or do what someone else wants you to do?" Because of the Hamans in my life and the Haman I have been, I have learned that we are going to be okay. God has worked in mighty ways through the pain of close friends leaving our church. God's Church is more resilient than I gave her credit for. After all, God's grace is big enough for all of us, including me and Rebecca.

## MELISSA HOFMEISTER

Melissa Hofmeister is an engaging speaker, writer and leader. She is an active part of Stadia's Bloom ministry and made *Christian Standard's* "Top 40 under 40." Melissa also works for Thrivent Financial, where she is passionate about helping Christians be wise with money, live generously and positively impact their community. In partnership with Stadia, Melissa and her husband Brian planted Lakepoint Church (lakepointmuskego.org) in Muskego, Wisconsin in 2012. Three years later they opened the Muskego Circle Community Center. They have three sons.

## WOLVES IN SHEEP'S CLOTHING

I like to mow the grass. There is nothing quite like getting out the old push mower. It is the place where physical endorphins from strenuous labor combine with the solitude of the machine's humming roar. As a mother of three boys, I get the luxury of defining the hum of the mower as my "quiet moment" of the day. It is so loud I can confidently wave children away without guilt. I. Can't. Hear. You.

In these moments, Jesus and I have some of our most reflective times. Times when I pause and ask, "How am I, really?" It is almost like Jesus is the counselor and the mower is one of those fancy couches. You can't get up until you've finished. Since I'm a "cup half full" type of woman, this time is often a reflection of the moments I've yet to celebrate in the prior week. "I can't believe we are actually church planting! I can't believe people are coming and lives are changing and I get to be a part of it!" But in the summer of 2014, I found myself in another place. "How could this happen? What are we going to do?" The tears began to flow, my chest began to heave and I'm not sure if the mower was able to drown out the sobbing. On that day I kept mowing longer than I needed to in the backyard.

Rewinding a few years prior to that tearful, grassy day, in October 2012 my husband Brian and I partnered with Stadia and a network of Milwaukee churches to plant Lakepoint Church in Muskego, Wisconsin. The city had great neighborhoods and schools but most people commuted elsewhere for work and entertainment. It was our vision to "Help People Connect to Jesus in Everyday Life, through Everyday Relationships." We wanted to create a community center for the city that could be a space for relationships to form and deepen. We envisioned cub scouts, fitness classes, home school groups, large scale social and cultural events—and a place to hold our services without having to set up a stage and chairs each week.

As church planters we didn't have the real estate background to take on a project like this, so we relied on an experienced team of business professionals from the church to start the search process. We looked at several properties but one location stood out far beyond the rest. It was a large property that had been vacant for a few years. The price had finally dropped within our budget as long as we sold a third of the location to a partner. Our loan couldn't be documented in time, so the committee drew up the terms and both parties signed on the deal in good faith.

While this was happening at a committee level, members of Lakepoint were praying and planning financially. We launched a capital campaign to share the vision, get feedback and allow others to partner with the financial commitment needed to see the community center become a reality.

Excitement mounted as we started displaying the drawings of our new location in the lobby of our current high school location each Sunday. The layout so perfectly arranged the right amount of space for children's rooms, an auditorium, a beautiful entrance and the location was easily accessible for people in our city.

Behind the scenes though, meetings became heated and good faith agreements began to crumble. The property and location was looking more and more financially lucrative to the other party involved. "If the church could just give up a little more space from the kids wing; if the church could just split the community room in two; if…" Things were getting uncomfortable, but surely everyone would stick to the original intent and, in the end, do what was right for the church. Right?

It was only five days until "Commitment Sunday"—the day when each family in the church hands in the prayerfully considered amount they plan to donate over the next two years. Brian came home in the middle of the day. He looked like he was going to throw up.

"It's over."

"What?"

"Stolen really. Hijacked. I don't even have words for it. They're changing the terms on us. They're taking enough space that it's no longer the community center we dreamed it would be, let alone the church we need it to be."

"Don't you have a signed agreement?"

"Yes. But the agreement was built on trust, so it's not legally binding. We'd be buried in legal fees trying to uphold a document signed in good faith. If our 'partners' want to take the building, there's nothing we can do but watch."

My stomach sank. "I need to mow the lawn."

There I was in the backyard, pushing the mower in circles, sobbing deeper than I had ever sobbed before. "Who could do such a thing? Against a church? Why would God let someone get away with this?" Our hopes had been strung along. I just couldn't understand how a good plan, from God, could be hijacked.

Maybe wolves were there all along and we just wanted to see sheep. Maybe in our passion for God's plan to come together, we ignored warning signs and allowed them in. Or maybe the world is full of wolves in sheep's clothing, and it's more about how we as a church respond. As I mowed, I was reminded of the story of Haman. He tried to stop God's plan to use the Hebrew people to bring redemption to the world. Instead, God used the looming genocide to build the faith of Esther, Mordecai and an entire people group.

We were at a crossroads. It wasn't just a handful of hurt people on a private planning team. We had to publicly talk this out with our congregation. In only five days, Brian would stand on the stage and ask families to commit to funding a building that God was calling us to create, while no longer knowing when or where that would be. Would the church trust God's call to build a community center in the midst of uncertainty? Would they believe God would provide an alternative location in the months to come?

Brian stood on the stage that Sunday and shared that the "terms of the agreement" for the proposed building had changed and that we would be looking for a new property. He reminded our church family that God's call was still true and the funds we were committing would put us in an even better position when the right opportunity came along. He didn't name names; he didn't show disgust. He spoke confidently, full of the Spirit, even though inside the hurt was terribly real. I prayed throughout that service for Brian's integrity to stand.

Haman walked the streets with a righteous air only days before his plan backfired on him. No, we never got our hanging—or any sense of justice for that matter—in the building project. We did, however, get to see the glory of God shine and His cause win out in the end.

On that "Commitment Sunday" our church stepped forward and pledged the exact amount of finances we would have needed as if the project were still going to happen. What an amazing response of faith, even when sight wasn't working! With humble hearts, our church family grew in dependence upon God—far more than if the easy road would have come to fruition. Together we still believed that this was God's church, God's city, and His heart for redeeming our city was much bigger than ours. God renewed our faith, just like Esther and her people, as we discovered God had more in store for us.

Against all hope, another property materialized months later. It took more than a year of negotiation, with the help of some good sheep who were in our corner this time. We now have a community center, where our church also meets on Sundays. Dozens of local clubs and organizations have made us their home. Hundreds from the community attend the events we host. And now, thousands in our community value and respect the presence of Jesus, through us, in part due to the physical location God always had in mind to provide for us.

The faith of our family and our church grew as we encountered wolves in sheep's clothing. We learned to be still in crisis, knowing that no matter how painful it may be in the moment, in the end, no evil can defeat God's plan. As David once said: "Be still before the Lord and wait patiently for him; do not fret when people succeed in their ways, when they carry out their wicked schemes (Psalm 37:7)."

There will be Hamans in ministry and in life. That is why we need times of solitude. It is these moments where you stop to 'mow the grass' and connect with God that define both your response as a person and as a leader guiding other sheep to a holy response.

**JENNIFER MURPHY**

Jennifer Murphy has worked in ministry for more than twenty-five years. She has served as the Director of Small Groups and Support & Recovery ministries and has a deep passion for pastoral care. Certified as a lay counselor, Jennifer is honored to be a Fellow with The Allender Center (theallendercenter.org) in Seattle, Washington where she comes alongside others in their stories of trauma and abuse. She loves to read, tries to write and always wants to engage in a good story. She is married with two young adult daughters and lives in the Chicago area.

## A SEAT AT THE TABLE

I walked into the room and found a chair at the far corner of the conference table set for 12. I sat down. I could not believe it. I finally had a seat at the table.

I was one of those children who hated the "kids table" at Thanksgiving and other family gatherings. I always wanted to join the adults to listen in on their conversations; but I also wanted to contribute, to share what I thought, to ask questions and to bring my point of view. I learned at a very early age, however, that while I could set and serve the table, the seats were already taken and reserved for people who did not look like me.

Like many middle school students I had the experience of standing with my lunch in the cafeteria desperately looking for a place to sit. Every time I shuffled up to an empty seat, the kids at the table would slide over and say, "You can't sit here!" As I would turn to walk away, I knew they were snickering and pulling their eyes into slits to mimic my Japanese features. Many times I took my lunch to the bathroom and ate alone in a stall. As I got on the bus kids would sing songs about my "yellow skin" as the bus driver would have to force kids to let me sit down so she could drive her route.

The shame of exclusion drove me to a self-sufficiency and hyper vigilance that, though exhausting, did have some benefits. I learned how to read a room, facing any situation like the books that held the stories I loved. I was hard working, responsible, dependable, and even-keeled. In high school and college these skills got me good grades and into positions of secondary leadership. I was the "secretary" or "treasurer," but I mostly saw white males at the top or center of every place of power and influence.

Despite my hope and expectation, the Church had been no different. I had been in ministry for more than 10 years when I sat down at that conference table in the pastor's office. I had been asked to be on the Governing Board of a large and expanding church where I had led and served in children's, women's and small group ministries for years. I was the first minority woman to be invited to this group of 12 and I took my seat with both gratitude and pride.

We began the meeting with introductions, with board member after board member listing their business or financial experience and stating how they were serving their second or third terms. When it was my turn I talked about pastoral care, leadership development, speaking truth and the power of sharing stories. The faces around me went blank with surprise or boredom. I ended quickly by saying, "But this is the first time I've been on a board, so I hope you will help me learn how I can contribute." Chuckles went around the room. Then, the Lead Pastor leaned in from the head of the table and said to me, "Honey, all you have to do is look down at me when it's time to vote. If I shake my head yes then vote yes, if I shake my head no, vote no."

I left that board after a tumultuous nine months. It became very clear I was not supposed to be there. I was the 'token' member who, in gratitude for being included, should simply follow directions and publically support everything and anything asked of me. My self-sufficiency and hyper vigilance, however, grew from experiences of being the outcast and created in me a hunger for justice, a passion for restoration and a commitment to seek and speak truth.

The church wanted to enter a building campaign in a manner that seemed financially and spiritually irresponsible. Leaders began pushing the agenda in ways that felt manipulative and deceitful, not unlike Haman. I not only refused to look down the table and vote according to a headshake, but I also asked a lot of questions, argued and made a fuss. I wish I could say that all of my actions came from honest, good places of conviction and discernment, but some of them did not. I felt angry, hurt and betrayed, but most of all I felt like a fool, also not unlike Haman.

I had allowed my desire to be empowered and included as someone of value lure me into a demeaning, patronizing situation and I felt small and stupid. To alleviate my shame, I vowed to make them pay. The board allowed me at the table because they needed to appear inclusive of women and minorities. They thought they were going to get a submissive and supportive board member who would sit quietly in the corner; but in my anger and pain, I decided to flip the table instead. I was going to be as intense and provoking as I could at every meeting, looking to challenge and expose. I don't know who was more relieved when I stepped down from the board, them or me.

I wish that table was the last time I faced the sting of patronizing patriarchy and the pain of humiliation for thinking I was valued and wanted, but it was not. And, I often still respond to being excluded or belittled by becoming closed off, despairing, bitter or self-righteous. It is so easy for me to turn contemptuous toward others or myself and let my heart grow hard. When you get "Hamaned" it is quite easy to "Haman" in return. To stay open and tender with my hopes and desires feels so foolish—like I am setting myself up for humiliation and disappointment again.

Psalm 23 paints a picture of God's goodness and grace that has both convicted and comforted my weary heart as I've wrestled with what it means to have a seat at the table. Verse 5 says of the Lord, "You prepare a feast for me in the presence of my enemies. You honor me by anointing my head with oil. My cup overflows with blessing" (NLT). As a Japanese-American woman with some prophetic gifts, I am not going to fit in easily to the North American Church. I can refuse to grieve the sorrow of that experience and instead ingest shame that turns me ugly and small. I can vengefully grab power and demand attention, but harm others while remaining insecure and alone. Or, I can dare to believe verse 5 of Psalm 23—there is a seat of honor and blessing set for me by the Living God at a banquet table in the midst of all the faces and voices who have said you do not belong, you do not matter, you are not wanted.

I am writing this during the month I will turn 50. I did not want a party, but my husband insisted and planned a dinner where there will be beautifully set tables with good food and drink for my friends. It's difficult for me to even imagine what that night will be like—to be in a room filled with people I love, who have reflected the heart of Jesus to me and who are there to celebrate my life. It is almost too much to bear. I believe, however, it is what we are made for—to have our unique place of blessing and honor. God created us to be included, known and loved.

Three days from now, like we see many times in the book of Esther, I will come to a banquet. Friends will have gathered around four large tables and at each one there will be an extra seat—especially for me.

## ROZELLA HAYDÉE WHITE

Rozella Haydée White is a life and leadership coach desperately seeking justice, mercy, humility and love. She is the owner of RHW Consulting (rozellahwhite.com), a boutique firm focused on accompanying people as they live their most meaningful life. She also serves as the Houston City Director for Mission Year (missionyear.org), an organization committed to walking with young adults as they love God and love their neighbor. Rozella is a writer, teacher, speaker and public theologian, boldly engaging issues of faith, justice, mental illness and the radical and transformative love of God as embodied in the person of Jesus. She believes everyone is gifted and has the power to transform themselves, their communities and the world when they tap into their most authentic self.

# EMBRACING YOUR SHADOW[6]

Just as Haman and Mordecai are described with clarity in the book of Esther, I am very clear about who I am and how I show up in the world. I carry major parts of my identity with me. I am black. I am a woman. These two realities are inescapable for me, and they were inescapable for Mordecai. He was a man. He was a Jew. I don't believe Mordecai would have wanted to be anyone other than who he was created to be. Neither do I.

My two realities of being black and being a woman mean something in every space I inhabit. They are visible and I believe that this is what makes conversations about race and gender slightly different than conversations about other issues of injustice. This is another way that I have learned to embrace my shadow—accepting my whole self.

The color of my skin and my gender orientation have statistically been shown to be characteristics that impact how I'm paid, how I'm educated, how law enforcement officers relate to me, how I receive medical treatment and a myriad of other issues. Personally, I could go into more detail about

---

6 Adapted from Rozella Haydée White's blog post "A Word to White People," https:// embracingmyshadow.com (March 11, 2017), posted on September 8, 2015.

how my gender and race impact my vocation in the Church, but I'll save that for another time. The bottom line, racism isn't just limited to my personal experiences—it is far-reaching and systemic. Haman didn't just seek to destroy one Jewish male named Mordecai, he sought to destroy all of Mordecai's people (Esther 3:6).

I'm also very aware of how my gender and race impact my relationships with black men. There is no doubt Mordecai's gender and race also impacted his relationships with others. Today there is a long history of the destruction of the black family, the destruction of the relationships between black men and women. It has continued to be a reality to my existence and the existence of many of my sisters. All of this to say: I am very clear about who I am and how I show up in the world—and what that means.

I was recently ranting to a dear friend about the current state of affairs of race in America, especially within the Church. At the time I was getting constant requests to lead discussions or workshops or give advice to well-meaning, white Christians who want to know what they can do about racism. I was going on and on to my friend about how I was tired of teaching and suggesting and providing information for people. Although I was not actually being asked to bow down like Haman asked Mordecai, this sudden influx of requests felt similarly harmful. More than humbling me, I felt humiliated and angry. At some point, my friend interrupted me and asked, "Roze, what do you want from white people?" In a very exasperated voice I said, "I want people not to be racists but I don't want to have to teach them!" To this my friend replied, "People genuinely don't know what to do."

I sighed at this response. And then something happened. My friend forced me to articulate what I wanted from white Christians. And this is where my understanding of who I am and how I show up in the world and what this means actually comes into play. What if someone had asked Mordecai, "What do you want from Haman?" I can imagine Mordecai saying, "I want Haman to stop focusing on me and start worshiping God instead, but I don't want to have to teach him!" What if someone had asked Haman, "What do you want from Mordecai?" and then he replied, "I want Mordecai to respect who I am and the role that I have in the Persian kingdom, but I don't want to have to teach him!" How would the question, "What do you want from _____?" change this story? How could it change your story or your calling?

No matter what job I've had in ministry, my race and gender are lenses through which I see everything. This means that no matter the context, I am going to speak up for issues of injustice, especially as they relate to race and gender, because it deals with who I am. To not do so would be to deny the person God created me to be and to do a disservice to my calling. I embody this reality and I have no choice but to make sure that every decision, every experience, every plan that is created keep gender and race at the forefront.

So what do I want from white Christians? If God wants to use me to help people who genuinely don't know what to do, then here is my advice. Begin viewing everything you do through the lens of race by asking yourself these questions:

- How do your plans seek to accomplish the goal of eradicating racism?
- How is your programming helping white people become aware of their privilege?
- How do the resources and opportunities you provide encourage white people to publicly stand up against injustice and call out racism?
- How do experiences you create and plan truly accompany people of color?
- How are you raising your children to understand the reality that people of color and white people live in two different worlds?
- What do you tell yourself when you find yourself at all white tables?
- Do you only engage with other white people personally or do you make it a point to cultivate intimate relationships that are mutual and reciprocal with people of color?
- Do you take it upon yourself to learn about issues of racial injustice or do you expect others to teach you?
- What would it look like if every waking moment called you into a deeper awareness and created the inescapable reality that being committed to eradicate racism, or any other -ism, is Gospel work?

I know it sounds like a lot of work. But this is what I do every day and have done every moment of my life. Are you willing to join me and others in the struggle? Are you willing to claim who you are and how you show up in the world and grapple with what this means? Are you willing to embrace your shadow?

ANONYMOUS

CHAPTER FIVE

# AHASUERUS
## WHAT ARE YOU AFRAID OF?

I absolutely love leading, especially in and through the church. I love everything about coming alongside of people and helping them grow in their relationship with God. I love looking at how Jesus led—how he made time for people, spoke with such incredible authority, yet was prayerful and humble as he extended such revolutionary love and grace to the outcast. I love trying to emulate Jesus' leadership as best as possible through the power of the Holy Spirit. But as much as I love leading, I also know my limits. I firmly believe I am at my best as a #2 leader. For all of you middle-school minded readers, take a moment to laugh at the bathroom reference, but when you're done please hear me out. I am designed by God to be a great #2.

Maybe I shouldn't make this distinction within leadership—after all, everyone has different wirings and can lead from within whatever gifts and personalities God has given. Why do we need to say #1 or #2, especially if I am a co-pastor? While Rich and I are clearly equal partners, these designations help me. I don't hear one as better or more significant than the other. Both are needed, especially within the church. Over the years I have learned a lot about myself and it has been good to find my sweet spot. I can fill the #1 role when needed, but I am at my best when leading alongside a #1. I like thinking ten steps ahead of the #1 and helping make his or her leadership better. I thrive on the details, the things that often go unnoticed until they are missed. I have a shepherd-prophet wiring and I serve best with an apostle, evangelist and/or teacher.[1] I need someone who can see the bigger picture, the vision, the God-sized dream that is most often heard in a still, small voice (1 Kings 19:11-13). That is the kind of #1 I need in order to thrive as a #2.

The Persian Empire also needed a great #1. Instead, they got King Ahasuerus. Ahasuerus literally means 'Mighty Man.'[2] This designation calls to mind places where "Luxury Dining" or "Upscale Restaurant" is written within the names of their businesses. In my experience, if you have to say 'luxury' or 'upscale' or 'mighty' in your title, you are anything but what you claim to be. Throughout the book of Esther the 'mightiness' of Ahasuerus is portrayed through detailed descriptions of his extravagance and excess.[3] One can't help but sense that the lavish words chosen by the writer of Esther to describe Ahasuerus were not actually intended as a compliment. Why would a presumably Jewish writer want to exalt a Persian king who drinks too much, doesn't know the law and can't seem to make any decision on his own? Instead, the writer presents a caricature of a king who needs his palace, his property and his people to make him feel powerful. After all he is 'mighty.'

Ahasuerus is the best example we have of an insecure leader ruled by fear—the worst kind of #1. He can't seem to make any decision by himself. He is surrounded with advisors who are often just as insecure and self-focused as he is, ones who will back him up and tell him what he wants to hear. When he does make quick decisions it is often out of embarrassment, needing to save face so that he is not dishonored publicly. He banishes a queen and passes an edict without thinking twice. He seems all too willing to give away his signet ring—perhaps not wanting the buck to stop with him in case his decisions go wrong. The only time we see Ahasuerus stopping to reflect on the past is when his insomnia forces him to do so. Even then, readers can't help but feel he is like a child wanting a story read to him at night. Insecure and afraid, Ahasuerus hides well behind a façade of royalty, but do not be mistaken—he is no 'Mighty Man.'

---

1 To learn more about the fivefold ministry of Ephesians 4:11-13, go to www.theforgottenways.org/what-is-apest.aspx

2 Betchel, *Esther*, 21.

3 Day, *Esther*, 114.

I have been blessed to have many #1s in my life who have truly been 'mighty.' My first was the Youth Pastor who gave me that "for such a time as this moment" when I was only a sophomore in high school. Many have followed in his steps. I am grateful for the godly, visionary, Spirit-led, inspiring #1s whom God has placed in my life. I am honored that I learned what this looks like by watching my own mother and father lead. And I am incredibly blessed that the most important #1 leader in my life is now my husband, my friend and my co-laborer at NewStory Church. Yes, Rich and I are co-pastors and equal partners, but I have no problem being a #2 to his #1. It's just how I'm wired.

Having had the opportunity to observe many different #1s other than Rich, I have also encountered several Ahasueruses. You don't see it at first; it takes time to discern. If you peel back the layers, however, many church leaders are ruled by fear—fear of failure, fear of letting people down, fear of not being enough, fear of being found out and the list goes on. As church planter Vanessa Pugh has said, "In ministry you often live life either in a fishbowl or on a pedestal, and both of these places end up putting you in a cage."[4] It is a cage locked by fear—one of the most crippling tools Satan uses to destroy the work of God in and through the Church today.

This is especially true for #1 leaders. Yes, fear can get me down, but when a #2 leader is insecure, she or he can glean from the courage, the inspiration and the Spirit-led humility of a good #1. When a #1 leader lives in fear, however, the reverse does not tend to happen and the entire ministry is infected. It is a slow infection—more like a cancer that can go undetected. But it reproduces quickly and tends to impact every part of the Body. I have seen fearful #1s struggle to make decisions, be easily influenced by popular opinion and hide behind their positions—just like Ahasuerus. Most of them don't even realize they are doing it—just like Ahasuerus. He is a frustrating character in the book of Esther, and in real life I have often been just as frustrated at the fearful #1s I have known.

Over time I have had to face two realities. First, I have grown to feel sorrow for fearful #1 leaders. I don't mean to be patronizing, but that's how I read Ahasuerus too. Most of these #1s would fight tooth and nail before

---

4 This comes from a message entitled, "The Fishbowl, the Pedestal and the Cage" that Vanessa Pugh gave at Stadia's Bloom Retreat in September of 2016.

admitting they are afraid or insecure. They are under attack and they don't even know it. I grieve that for them. Second, I have had to turn and face myself. Am I pulling the wool over my own eyes too? Where am I insecure? How am I afraid? And is this cancer reproducing through me into our church? The church planting women whose stories fill the pages of this last section have faced their own obstacles of fears and insecurities within themselves, their churches and their neighborhoods. Whether or not they identify as more of a #1 or #2 leader, all of them have had to break through the façade of ministry to become women that God names 'mighty.'

**KIMBERLY BOLDEN**

Kimberly Bolden hails from the multi-cultural Caribbean nation of Trinidad & Tobago. Born to a Jamaican mother and Trinbagonian father, diversity, and reconciliation have been lifelong commitments for her and an essential part of her personal narrative. Kim and her husband Wesley reside on the Southside of Atlanta where they lead and serve Tri-Cities Church (tri-citieschurch.com)—a Stadia-partner, multi-ethnic Christian community. Prior to Tri-Cities Church, she served as a Ministry Fellow with Christian Union at Princeton University where she equipped Ivy-League students from across the world with tools to boldly live out their faith in all spheres of influence. At present, Kimberly works alongside a competent team at CrimsonInk (crimsonink.com)—a premiere printing and publication company based in Atlanta. She enjoys photography, coffee shops and outdoor adventures with her husband.

## THE DISEASE TO PLEASE[5]

Ever since I was a little girl, I had a knack for numbers and a knack for talking…out of turn most of the time. People were often impressed by how much I knew, and the more they were impressed, the more I kept talking. I loved the attention. I loved the affirmation until I realized it held me hostage from living my life. Like King Ahasuerus, I wanted people to like me.

The disease to please ensured that the word "No" was nowhere to be found in my personal vocabulary. I bent over backward to ensure others were accommodated at the expense of my time, relationships, health, and peace of mind. I allowed people's opinions to compromise my integrity because I found myself saying "Yes" when I really meant "No." I now realize there were even times I missed God's leading. My ears were pinned more to the loud utterings of the opinionated rather than the gentle whispers of God throughout the day.

---

5 Adapted from Kimberly's blog post "The Disease to Please," http://www.kimspeaksup (March 6, 2017), posted on August 28, 2015.

When I turned 30, I resolved to no longer live my life to please others, but to honor God and my family in my decisions. It was the only way to ensure that I gave my best "Yes." I am grateful for a husband who does not pressure me into things I do not want to do, but encourages me to say "No" even when it comes to church and ministry. Learning to say "No" has been so freeing and I am so grateful for my husband's support.

I have learned that the disease to please ultimately kills your joy. Always saying "Yes" forces you to live out someone else's blueprint rather than the one God has purposed for you. It's a miserable and unfulfilled life when we constantly try to please fickle and confused hearts. People may become agitated and annoyed by your "No." A mature and balanced leader, however, is able to discern whether the rejection is targeted to the request or to the person who asks. Most often the former is true. If it is the latter, there is a deeper issue.

So how do I discern my best "yes"? There are a few questions that I ask myself before I make commitments:

- Why? Who benefits?
- Will I complain while doing this? Do I really want to do this?
- What are their motives? What are my motives?
- Am I trying to prove anything by saying "yes"?
- Is this the best use of my resources? Am I the most competent option to complete this task?
- Am I compromising my integrity? Am I lying? Am I being fair?
- Am I balanced in my thoughts? How will this affect me emotionally?
- Will this cause me distress? Is this a life or death situation?
- Will the purpose of the task still be accomplished if I did not participate?
- Is there a better alternative instead of me? Have they exhausted all their options?
- Is this constructive criticism or manipulation?
- Is their request or my response laced with greed, pride or jealousy?
- Will I be ok if I am not acknowledged for my work?
- Is God glorified?

Whether or not you are a church planter, I recommend that everyone takes the time to answer these questions. You will be happy you did and your family and friends will, too.

The disease of Ahasuerus, the disease to please, adversely affects the heart and can only be combated through having a right perspective of God and yourself. God does not need us to accomplish His purposes throughout the earth but has chosen to use us. Despite what many may think, you are not a savior. The humbling reality is this: Life will go on without you. We do, however, desperately need a Savior to live with purpose. One of the keys to a purpose-filled life is not doing all the things, but doing the few things God has placed before you well. Saying "Yes" to everything squanders our best "Yes" to the right thing.

You, my friend, cannot be all things to all people. The only one well qualified for that job is God. Let God do His job and you do yours.

## SHANNON SMITH

Shannon Smith was raised all over the place, but she claims Crowley, Louisiana because that is where she spent most of high school and because the Cajuns have the best food. Graduating from Kentucky Christian University, Shannon went on to teach high school mathematics in Virginia. After thinking they would never have kids, God blessed Dan and Shannon with Zion (age 13), Azlan (age 12), and Journey (age 9). In 2005, Shannon and Dan moved to Cleveland, Ohio to start Momentum Christian Church (momentumchurch. com). It's been an adventure ever since! Shannon is currently the Small Groups Director at Momentum. She also helps lead worship at one of their campuses, hosts a small group and works to help the public schools by serving on the PTA. Shannon loves speaking to women of all ages and is passionate about loving God, loving people and making disciples who make disciples—all while wearing her heels and drinking a chai!

## WEAK AND MIGHTY

The Leopard Room in The Shark Club was known for its many billiard tables, dark décor, cigar smoke and caged female dancers. This is where my husband Dan and I would start a new young adult ministry as part of New Life Christian Church. We had the entire room, including the bartender, to use to bring young adults to Jesus every Sunday night. The adventure was exciting, scary and edgy all at the same time. We had a launch team, marketing plan and talent. We brought in energetic bands, skilled teachers and an out-of-town comedian. We arrived at The Shark Club early and stayed late. Week after week we provided a fantastic, trendy atmosphere for people to hear about Jesus.

After one year of intensive work, exhausting hours, and lots of planning with little to show for it, Dan and I were calling it quits on the bar ministry we had excitedly started. The young couple praised for their talent, academic success and leadership abilities had not been able to make it work. We had failed. I was embarrassed and tired, yet also relieved.

I was anything but 'mighty.' Fear of failure has always been one of my biggest weaknesses. At times it makes me push too hard. Other times it cripples me from exploring and developing the woman God made me to be. In the midst of mourning the death of our bar ministry dream, I confessed to Dan there was no way we would ever plant a church on our own. Never! So we metaphorically plugged our ears and repeated, "LaLaLaLaLaLa" over and over to avoid hearing any such calling. Insecurity set in and the fear of possibly failing paralyzed me. Florence Nightingale said, "How very little can be done under the spirit of fear." It would be four years before we would step out on faith again.

God patiently waited as we healed and began to learn from our failure. We had been overly confident in thinking our ministry would grow through shallow things—an edgy venue, fresh acts, being young, marketing strategies and more. We didn't forget about God. But like the luxuries of King Ahasuerus, we liked our "cool" things and depended on them too much. It's been said that failure is a great teacher and that is no joke. I know, however, that we aren't the only ones who have fallen into this trap.

I've had church planters tell me they became alcoholics because they chose to have alcohol at every event for people who don't follow Jesus. I've met planters who relied only on postcard marketing without actually getting out to meet people in their city or town. There are distracted, trend-focused planters with churches who jump on board every new fad that comes along in the church planting world without counting the cost. Then there are the planters who refuse to ask for help or listen to advise because they don't think they need it. I think many of us church planters are more like King Ahasuerus than we'd care to admit.

As for me, the time finally came to deal with my fear of failure. After four years Dan and I slowly took our fingers out of our ears as the calling to plant a church became apparent. It's funny how failure and a few extra years can humble a person. We went into our church plant with a good dose of healthy fear. Not the kind that paralyzes you, but the kind that makes you wholly and humbly dependent upon God, His calling, His mercy and His mission.

I had to come face to face with my insecurity and weaknesses and decide to push through with God's help. I had to let my fear of failure give birth to courage. As the axiom goes, "Courage is not the lack of fear, but the action in spite of fear." I needed to remember this with every obstacle we experienced in the process of planting a church. Three months before moving we lost our money to start our new church, we had to change the location of where our family would live, and the church would be located in a much more diverse demographic. Every apparent obstacle gave my courage a good workout.

Those initial workouts were vital, and they were just the beginning. Starting a church is actually the easy part, sustaining it is the hardest. We are now 12 years in, and it's in these sustaining years where I have seen fear and insecurity rear their ugly heads again and with greater force. The first time attendance dropped, the time offerings were frighteningly low and all spending had to stop, the awful day a launch team family we loved no longer wanted to be part of the church—and the list goes on. I cried as I talked to God about the decision to raise three children in an urban area with an inadequate public school system to be light in the darkness. It is in these times we are reminded of God's calling on our lives—that nagging force that continually calls us to God's mission in a specific way and in a certain direction. It is God's calling that gives us the courage to keep going.

That courage is how God has developed me beyond my weaknesses and fears. 2 Timothy 1:7 says, "For God gave us a spirit not of fear but of power and love and self-control" (ESV). I have had to fight through all of my fears—the fear of failure, the fear of missing opportunities and the fear of letting others down. As I've fought these fears God has grown power, love and self-discipline in me and in our church.

As a church leader I have had to talk to women about their sex lives, challenge small group leaders with tithing, ask leaders to step down and make other hard decisions that I know won't sit well with others. I mentor future leaders when I barely feel adequate, meet and care for my neighbors even though time is hard to come by and have confrontational meetings where people get to tell me how I let them down. It is this daily grind of church planting that I wouldn't change for the world because I know God has chosen me "for such a time as this." I know God sees all of my fears, insecurities and weaknesses and still believes I am 'mighty' and can make a difference in the kingdom. It is in my weakness God is strong (2 Corinthians 12:10)!

**KRISTA EVANS**

Krista Evans is an outgoing, well spoken, plays-with-herbs, nature lover who enjoys reading and give hugs to everyone she encounters. Krista is recently Finding her Forty (finding40.net) and has a new perspective on life and what's important! Krista is married to Marques "Big Cleve" Evans who is the pastor of Revolution 216 (www.revolife.org), a Stadia-partner church plant in Cleveland, Ohio. Together they have four fantastic children who all enjoy working out together, family game nights and walking in the park.

## BEING WHO I AM MADE TO BE

The moment you realize you've gone through life and haven't yet fulfilled any of your life goals is disheartening. One of my most painful experiences was listening to older individuals reflecting on their lives and how they didn't fulfill any of the goals they had for themselves. To hear these people share, with tearful eyes, about not ever knowing their purpose scared me! How does this happen?

I honestly do not think these people gave up on their goals intentionally. Once you become content with your life it is easy for dreams to fade. Once you start working a consistent, reliable job goals can become a distant glance. Our culture has a checklist that implies success—married, careers, house, car, and yearly vacations. When did these things begin to define who we are and become the goals for our lives?

I'm reminded of my grandfather who served this country, married and had children. He worked and retired from the steel mill, living his entire life with a 3rd-grade education and never really knowing how to read. My grandfather was a great man. He was kind to everyone he met, he was honest, he provided for his family, yet he could not read. He lived his life as if he never really had time to learn how to read. Although he lived in a different generation, is that any excuse? He lived a very fulfilling life but died never knowing how to read.

I share my grandfather's story to make the point that we cannot live our lives with excuses. What is it that prevents many people from accomplishing their goals? What keeps us from discovering our purpose? When the obstacles come, do they become excuses for us not to succeed? Each of us has a story to be told.

I had always been satisfied with being average. I was fine with never having the name 'mighty one,' like Ahasuerus. I knew I had gifts and talents, but I was working, being a wife, mother and just living in my daily routine. My husband, thankfully, began challenging me—he knew I had more in me. I also began to be tested at work and in my faith community. As an only child, I now had the responsibility of caring for an ill parent. I seemed to be facing challenges in every area of my life, and it was one of the most difficult times I've ever experienced.

It was through these difficulties and the words of my husband that I began to see more of myself. I began to discover the kind of person I am, how I had treated others, the jobs I had acquired and how we were raising our children. I don't know why I was challenged "for such a time as this," but it made me want to live differently. I wondered, "What was my Heavenly Father trying to tell me and show me?"

While I was uncovering both good and bad qualities about myself I had never noticed before, I realized I had not even begun to tap into my full potential in many areas of my life. I can't say I wanted more, but I expected more of myself. With those expectations, however, came more resistance. The resistance I felt was mostly internal. I began to question everything about myself. I doubted who I was and questioned if I was capable of doing better or even having better things. Why was I not happy with what I had and where I was? Matthew 19:26 Jesus says, "With man this is impossible, but with God all things are possible." Imagine the possibilities if I trusted the One who made everything.

Fear of change is real. I was content with who I was, but then things started to change. I wanted and expected more from myself. I had become my worst critic and self-doubt was a terrible hindrance. I doubted myself for so long that I didn't even know how to change. My outside world appeared all together, but there was an internal struggle that was causing me to question everything. I had to trust an Almighty Father who is capable of anything, and now I have a weapon to win! I was no longer content to be like Ahasuerus!

Change didn't happen overnight; it was a process. I first had to trust God enough to admit I couldn't fight this alone. I decided to allow God to guide me in every way so I could live to my full potential. I began to see, through visions and intuition, what I should be striving toward and what to abandon. I no longer questioned every decision, but grew in faith and boldness as I trusted and followed God. It felt great! I never left room for doubt or fear to come in at all. If I even began to question something God had told me, I reminded myself that I could do this.

Finding my purpose is not a final destination, it's my way of life. Living on purpose is a daily action I am choosing. My desire is to look back at my life and be able to tell stories of all the things I've tried and accomplished. I want to look back and know that I've served, helped and loved others to the best of my ability. I want to keep throwing off the Ahasuerus in me and be who I am made to be!

## MANDY SMITH

Originally from Australia, Mandy Smith is the lead pastor of University Christian Church (universitychristianchurch.net), a campus and neighborhood congregation with its own fair-trade café in Cincinnati, Ohio. She is also the creator of The Collect, a citywide trash-to-art project, for which she was named one of Cincinnati's Coolest People by *CityBeat Magazine*. Mandy loves Jesus' invitation to be like children and often wonders how that looks in a world of email and traffic jams. Her favorite questions are "Would you like a cup of tea?" and "How can I help you?" With the help of many friends and many cups of tea, she spends her days leading her church, raising her kids and supporting her husband in his ministry as a New Testament Professor. Her most recent book is *The Vulnerable Pastor: How Human Limitations Empower Our Ministry* (ivpress.com/the-vulnerable-pastor).

## LEADING LIKE A CHILD[6]

Following your childlike heart works when you are on sabbatical. During my eight weeks with nothing to do, I sensed God saying, "Just be like a child." So with God's blessing, I took my time napping, lying in the grass and eating my favorite things. I sensed there was something significant in this childlikeness and that it wasn't only a lesson for sabbatical. So now that I'm back at work, I'm asking, "How do I lead meetings and write sermons like a child?"

I've been pondering that question for a while now and today something fell into place as I prepared this week's sermon on Solomon. As he prays his famous prayer, asking for wisdom to rule well, Solomon says, "Now, Lord my God, you have made your servant king in place of my father, David. But I am only a little child and do not know how to carry out my duties" (1 Kings 3:7).

---

6 For this chapter Mandy Smith adapted an article entitled "The Wise Child King" from Christianity Today's Leadership Journal website, http://www.christianitytoday.com/pastors/2015/december-web-exclusive/wise-child-king.html (December 2015).

As a great king of Israel, growing up in the courts of King David, Solomon was groomed for this, yet instead of a king, he feels like a child. I wonder if that day and that prayer were in Solomon's mind when compiling these words in Proverbs, "The fear of the Lord is the beginning of wisdom" (Proverbs 9:10).

Knowing who God is—and that it's not us—forces us to ask questions and seek insight from God and others. In so doing, we gain wisdom—the kind of wisdom that helps us know how to go about our duties and what the next step should be. The kind of reverence that shows us how big God is and how small we are, becomes the beginning of wisdom. But it's a never-ending beginning, reminding us of how small we are every time we return to our need for the Lord.

How do we, as leaders, usually respond when we feel like children? Our work will inevitably take us to the place Solomon is when he says he's like a child. Faced regularly with church needs that are beyond us: a heart beyond our repairing; a passage of scripture beyond our understanding; a ministry challenge beyond an easy fix. The question is, "How will we respond when we feel inadequate and incompetent, when the issues are bigger than the answers and when we can't control outcomes?"

Over one year ago my church found itself in the middle of a neighborhood in crisis. You may have seen the news stories about the shooting of an unarmed black man, Samuel Dubose, after a routine traffic stop which took place just a few streets from my church. On the day of the hearing for the police officer accused of killing him, the nearby university closed its campus and there was tension in the air. Will justice be served? Will there be unrest in our streets?

I have to admit I felt like a child. I knew the church should do something, but I had no idea how to respond. I didn't know how it felt to be a black member of our community that day. I didn't know the best way to foster community-building or real peace. I felt like a child. And it didn't feel right. I wanted to understand and control. This situation, however, was beyond me. So I did all I could think to do: call a few folks and say, "What should we do?"

Without any concrete plans, we kept the building open all night, not knowing what to expect. It felt insubstantial and unprofessional to have such an unstructured response, but it became something beautiful as church and community members gathered and helped shape what the night would become. One community member started playing hymns on the piano, an intern set up prayer candles, a few people brought art supplies and someone made a prayer-journaling table.

Throughout the night around 75 church and community members talked about their pain and prayed for peace. Something happened that night that showed me it's okay to be a child. Being like a child had led me to invite others because I knew I couldn't do it alone. Being as a child forced me to ask questions, which helped me become a better leader, even though I didn't feel much like a leader.

Katy Smith, the Minnesota Teacher of the Year, shares what she's learned from toddlers about leadership. "I stand in awe of how unapologetic they are about their approach to life. They are messy, impulsive and uninhibited." We value the playfulness of children, but hearing her experiences with children made me see how very serious their example can be for us. Small children trust their instincts. They bring their whole selves and engage with honesty, integrity, and courage.

Toddlers are unashamed to be fully themselves in front of other people and to be found without an easy answer. They are prolific creators, continually trying new things, even if it doesn't always work out as planned. They are not afraid to say hard or joyful things. They will let you know when they're hurting, they know how to ask for help and don't see emotions as weakness. They know what they need in hard times and find resources to get them through. They are both self-confident and okay with the fact that they sometimes need others. Perhaps the thing we can learn most from them and ourselves as children—is how to be comfortable with our humanness.

Next time I'm faced with my human limitations, I hope I remember the potential in it. I hope I remember to overcome a lifetime of learning to control and direct. I hope I learn the kind of wisdom Solomon had that Ahasuerus didn't—the kind that knows its limits.

But Solomon is both a positive and negative example. He knew how to seek God from childlikeness. But as we see later in Solomon's story, he became puffed up in his strength and resources and lost that childlike sense of his need for God. It might be easy to think he went from being like a child to being an adult.

In fact, he went from childlikeness to childishness. Ahasuerus, on the other hand, had more childishness throughout his reign. Childishness stomps its feet, demands its way, trying to control beyond its reach. So how do we avoid childishness and protect childlikeness? Like Solomon, when our job is new it's easy to know we're children. When we've done the job for years and we're confident in our strength, however, we must find ways to retain a healthy sense of our smallness. Let's learn from both Solomon and Ahasuerus and begin to lead in the best of ways—like a child.

ANONYMOUS

# WHAT'S IN A NAME?

As a pastor, I have attended, participated in and officiated many weddings throughout my twenty years of ministry. There is one wedding I will never forget, although my memory of it has nothing to do with the lovely couple married that day. During the rehearsal of my cousin's wedding, I sat in a pew next to my grandmother waiting for my part to come. I was to read Scripture during the ceremony and the coordinator wanted to check my microphone and ensure that I knew my cue. My training in high school as the Program Team Leader in our youth group had prepared me well. As I sat next to Granna, I will never forget listening to her read the program quietly to herself. She paused as she reached my name, slowly reading "Dori." She looked at me and said, "My name is kind of like that. My name is Doris."

My eyes teared up as a lump formed in my throat. "That's right, Granna, Doris is your name," I said. Perhaps I should have stopped there, in gratitude that her Alzheimer's was still at the stage where she could remember her name and talk to me. But her diagnosis was new at the time, so I continued, "Dori is me, Granna. I am Dori, but my real name is Doris." I squeezed her hand as my voice cracked. My strong, deep voice could barely add the words "I am named after you." At this point in her disease I never knew if I should correct her or simply sit with her in the haze of uncertainty. On this day, however, something stirred within me, prompting me to remind her of who I was, specifically who I was in relation to her. I am not named after Doris Day; I was not named after a fish in a famous animated film. I am named after Doris Rhame and I wanted her to know my name. I was looking for recognition for the purpose of relationship.

Years later, under much different circumstances, I had another significant conversation about my name. I was leaving a position at a church and tears were filling my eyes in a different way than they had with Granna. Though not an exact quote, "You'll never make a name for yourself" was the threat handed to me on that day. This was one of the final words said to me at the end of an unforgettably sad conversation. These words have haunted me in a way that I have hated. I honestly don't think I ever aspired to "make a name for myself" until I was told on that day that I wouldn't. Isn't that how it works? What begins as a competitive spirit gives birth to pride. Tell me I can't do something and then all of a sudden I want to do it. But just as that threat should have never been launched at me, I must stop letting it whisper to me. The person who said it is not my audience. No one person is. The only audience that matters is Jesus.

There is no approval or applause that can give me what God can give. We are promised in Revelation 2:17 that the victorious ones in Jesus will be given "a white stone with a new name written on it, known only to the one who receives it." My name, not in bright lights, not for all the world to see. My name given to me by the One who created me on something small enough to fit in my pocket. My name written in the book of life through the blood of the Lamb. My name given to me not for the purpose of recognition, but through the gift of relationship.

The 21 women, including myself, whose stories make up this book have been named and pictured, with bios given, not for the purpose of fame or adoration. I believe all of them would agree that the last thing any of us need is to be put on another pedestal. Ministry provides enough false platforms that Jesus works overtime to tear down in us. Rather, I want to recognize these women for the purpose of relationship. Most of them I know personally and some of them I am just starting to get to know. But I don't mean their relationship with me—I mean their relationship with the Church. Will the churches they have sweated for, cried for and bled for (stopping short of a literal plasma donation) recognize them and name them? Will your church recognize all of the people who have contributed, served and volunteered for the sake of sharing the good news of Jesus to the glory of God?

Of all the people we have discussed in this book—Vashti, Esther, Mordecai, Haman and Ahasuerus—there is One we all can relate to in the book of

Esther. At the risk of arrogance, I think women in ministry can uniquely relate to God in Esther. Of course, all of us fall short of the glory of God, but when it comes to the apparent absence of God in the book—being unnamed yet undeniably significant, remaining anonymous yet clearly present—that is where women in ministry can relate. And that is where we must remind each other: no matter your story, you have a name in ministry. You may not know this because you may not feel like you fit with the title "pastor." You may not know this because you've had a title but had to "stick with the men" when it comes to ministry. Today, I want to invite every woman to boldly "stick with the women." There is a seat at God's table for all of us—stay-at-home moms, marketplace workers, support staff, volunteers and pastors. Regardless of title, you have a name. God wants to give you a name in this church planting world. One of the ways I have found a seat at the table is through Stadia's Bloom ministry. You may find your place there too, or somewhere else, but I hope you find it. I hope you find a place God uses to name you well.

As I sit here writing the conclusion to this book, I have music playing in the background on Pandora™ radio. If you're not familiar with this free online streaming service, it is similar to the radio—listeners don't pick what song plays next. I pick the station but the song choices are seemingly random. I say "seemingly" because as I wrote that last paragraph a song came on with a repeated phrase that took my breath away. Over and over throughout the song I kept hearing, "He knows your name." Again, I find my eyes tearing up as I look up the song and learn that it's by a group called Esterlyn and the song is entitled, "Esther." Seriously. I'm not making this up—I'm not that creative.

My desire as a church planting woman is to walk a fine line. How do I find my voice, find my significance and make an impact in a world that often doesn't hear or recognize me? At the same time, my goal cannot be to make a name for myself. That is something only God can do. God is in the business of naming me and naming all of us. So no matter how anonymous we may seem or feel at times—we have a place in the kingdom of God, and our true King is waiting to show us what that place is and what our name is. Will you let God name you?

What's in a name? Everything, yet nothing, at the same time. A name given by God is everything. A name given by pride, self-promotion and insecurity is nothing. So, to the women reading the final page of this book: What is your true name today? I encourage you to sit at the feet of Jesus with your own stories and ask him to name you. And to the men who have dared to pick up this book and spend time with our stories, thank you for humbly listening. I hope you will take the next courageous step by asking, "Who should I name today?" Then sit with your own stories at the feet of Jesus and see who he brings to your mind. May all of us—women and men alike—turn to Jesus with these questions, asking not for sake of recognition, but for the sake of relationship.

# ACKNOWLEDGEMENTS

*The boundary lines have fallen for me in pleasant places; surely I have a delightful inheritance.*

— Psalm 16:6

In addition to Granna, my full namesake includes Grandma Hauk. This reminds me of the heritage of faith I stepped into when I was born. While not perfect, my grandparents, parents, siblings and extended family have given me story after story of faithfulness in the midst of struggle, guidance in the midst of uncertainty and laughter—always laughter. Gary and Brenda Hauk—thank you for the endless hours you have listened to me, processed with me and challenged me to new perspectives. You inspire me and I am proud to call you Mom and Dad. I love you more.

God used numerous people at my home church in Franklin, Tennessee to shape me, encourage me, support me and ordain me as a minister. To name a few—thank you Kathryn Seay, Jordan Blanton, Canaan Sanders, Leah Hitson, Amanda Martin, Dick Wells, Rick White, Rachel Jones, Dixie Inman, Tad Wilson, Dave Felty, Dianne Cobb, Kent and Karen Williams, Kristy Collins, Donna Wilson, Doc Watson, Rob Warren, Mary and Drew Thigpen, Bill and Barbara Ladshaw, Paula Palermo, Carey Miller, Chuck and Connie Gartman, Richard and Mary Barnes and Darren Whitehead.

Thank you Baylor University for being the place where I began to build pigeon-holes for all of my questions. Thank you Dr. Rosalie Beck for shaping my view of women in ministry with wisdom, humble strength and a love of

Scripture. Thank you Compassion Christian Church in Savannah, Georgia for taking a risk on a year-long intern. Thank you Paul and Julia Wingfield, Doug Hartley, Randall Tonini, and all the staff and ministry volunteers for pouring into me and serving alongside me. Thank you Richard and Nancy Gorman, Sarah Huxford and Mike Frazier for the significant role you played in my friendship with Rich. Thank you Indu Lall for seeing what I couldn't see on that mission trip to India.

Thank you Emmanuel Christian Seminary for providing a safe, courageous place for me to bring my many pigeon-holes and begin figuring out what goes where. During my time in Johnson City, I am also grateful for my "second professors," the residents of the John Sevier Center and the ragamuffin group of people who made up The Melting Pot Church.

Thank you Tom and Debbie Jones and all of the Stadia family for introducing us to church planting and naming us in a new way. In addition to Stadia, thank you to the people and churches who helped finance, support and start NewStory Church; getting to where we are today was the biggest challenge of my life. I am sorry that it came at such a high cost, but I am grateful for God's grace and for the lessons I learned and continue to learn. Thank you NewStory for being my family in Chicago. Thank you for the time and forgiveness you extended to me as I wrote this book. Thank you Qiana Tate, Josh Hurley, Liz Gentry and the NewStory Direction and Discernment Team for leading our church to follow Jesus.

Thank you to the 2016 NewStory Women's Group for helping me first discover how the book of Esther connected with church planting women. Sue Lueders and Cortney West, leading that group with you is something I will never forget. Johndalyn Armstrong, Faith Walls, Rozella Haydée White and Leah Anderson—thank you for being patient with me as I try, yet continually fail, to understand what it would be like to walk in your shoes.

Thank you Allender Center, Jen Murphy, Hannah Seppanen and my Lay Counseling group for helping me hear Jesus name me at my best as a wise, Spirit-led, warrior-child who fights with hope.

Thank you Debbie Jones for asking me to write a book. God's timing is threaded throughout our journey together and within the journey of Bloom. You have become one of my biggest encouragers and your words have kept me going. Thank you Sara McGue for compiling all of these stories and responding to my many texts and phone calls to help make this thing happen. I am thankful for you as another "woke" church planting woman. Thank you to all of the writers who risked sharing their stories in this book, especially the women of color. Thank you Amanda Pavich and Amy Jackson for jumping in during the final stretch to help me see this thing through to the end. Thank you Lena Masek for using your eye for details and incredible graphic design gifts to make me look better than I am.

Of course, I say all of this, knowing I owe so much gratitude to one person. Rich Gorman you are my best friend and my partner. I can't believe I get to call you my husband too. I am the luckiest, Meir Ja'an. Thank you for the time, work and energy you continually sacrifice because you believe the best in me and still love the worst in me. You are the strongest man I know. Thank you for loving the strong woman in me with your 'crazy eyes.' Charis and Nia, you have the best Daddy. He will not be perfect but he is good. Thank you girls for simply being born. No matter what the world tells you, you are enough. Thank God for making you enough.

Thank you, Lord, for making me enough. Thank you, Lord, for naming me and continuing to reveal more of your Name to me. Just as I am never anonymous to You, may You never be anonymous to me.

ANONYMOUS

ABOUT THE AUTHOR

# DORI GORMAN

Dori Gorman is the co-founder and co-pastor of NewStory Church (newstorychicago.com), a Stadia-partner church on the north side of Chicago, Illinois. She holds a BA from Baylor University, and a Masters of Divinity from Emmanuel Christian Seminary. She is

Photo by Spencer Hall

gifted as a shepherd-prophet, with a passion for preaching, discipleship and coming alongside the forgotten. Dori has pioneered several initiatives in Chicago, including a fundraising organization for Swift Elementary School and an after-school club for middle school students. She is honored to partner with Stadia's Bloom ministry to help women maximize their role in starting churches. In her free time, she loves to read, rock climb, play basketball and have fun with her family—Rich, Charis and Nia.